NOW YOU SEE ME!

NOW YOU SEE ME!

AN INTRODUCTION TO 100 YEARS OF BLACK DESIGN

CHARLENE PREMPEH

PRESTEL

MUNICH · LONDON · NEW YORK

CONTENTS

Part 3: Graphic Design

nOW YOU SEE ME
INTRODUCTION

WORDS BY
CHARLENE PREMPEH

I founded the agency arm of A Vibe Called Tech in the summer of 2020 amidst the collective chaos of a pandemic and a reckoning on the treatment of Black Lives sparked by the death of George Floyd that May. The original intent of the agency was to celebrate Black creativity. It has since evolved to include all marginalized communities under a collaborative ethos that necessitates brainstorming sessions with partners and friends across media, art, and design. It was in one such meeting that I was first introduced to Ann Lowe. We were working on a brief for the North Face X Gucci collection and wanted to connect the explorer aesthetic to stories of past Black pioneers. Chrystal Genesis, founder of culture podcast Stance, and Lewis Gilbert, creative director at A Vibe Called Tech, were exuberantly flinging names around on a Zoom call when Genesis asked, "What about Ann Lowe? The woman who designed Jackie Kennedy's wedding dress?" I am not a Jackie Kennedy obsessive but given the level of attention that has been paid to her every outfit, I felt like I should know the name. "How come I've never heard of her?" spilled from my mouth before I had time to scoop it back in. A pause, then ironic laughter followed by a response delivered in chorus: "Why do you think?"

For decades, Black designers have been sheathed in an invisible cloak. The absence of prestige and recognition afforded to Black figures in this space has shapeshifted as the formality of segregation and colonial rule has given way to more subtle forms of gatekeeping and erasure. With unprecedented levels of attention being paid to diversity in creative fields, debates on the need for representation have expanded—and finally burst—to unveil a new, more vibrant discussion about economic sustainability for Black designers, access to design industries, and support for emerging talent.

This appetite for evolution is noticeably strong in the fields of fashion, architecture, and graphic design. All three boast a rich history of Black makers, and there is mounting urgency for that legacy to be honored, as well as for today's Black designers to be given the attention and respect they deserve. Transforming the lens through which Black designers of past and present are viewed involves asking crucial questions about creative freedom, the power dynamics of the design world, and what it means to create in a field where Black is perceived as an aesthetic positioning.

Though what I am alluding to is a certain proclivity for the Black designer to be boxed in, I am also intrigued by the creative dexterity that comes from a lineage of making that has existed either literally and/or culturally on the fringes of mainstream white society. It raises larger, more philosophical debates about the distinction between self-expression and circumstance, about creative autonomy and societal structure, and ultimately an inquiry of what it means to create when your Blackness is inescapable.

During the past century there have been symbolic developments for Black people globally. With the signing of the Civil Rights Act in 1964, African Americans could no longer be legally segregated. Across the Atlantic, Ghana became the first sub-Saharan country to gain independence from the British Empire in 1957, sparking a tsunami of independence movements across the continent. More recently, the global Black Lives Matter protests forced industry and the wider public to consider the ways in which our society remains racist. While none of these events immediately resolved the layered prejudices that have been systematically inflicted upon the Black community for generations, overall, they signify a moving tide toward equality. The changes have also shone a light on the complexities of navigating a career as a Black person in white-dominated industries: Do you work within the establishment to create change, or should you prioritize success in your own community? Who are the gatekeepers influencing the trajectories of Black people and what power do they wield? How does a Black person escape the shackles of tokenism and monolithic ideas of the Black experience? The business of design, an industry synonymous with liberalism and progression, is the ideal space to observe the dilemmas raised by these changes and the real-world impact on Black lives.

The question posed by Gilbert and Genesis on that fateful Zoom call led me down a rabbit hole which has thrown up as much delight as it has stunned outrage. This book is the first stage of unpacking that experience. My aim is to give an introduction to Black design from the past hundred years in an attempt to identify some of the ways the space has evolved in relation to Blackness. What you will not find in these pages is a comprehensive survey. There are many Black designers who have worked and are working across fashion, architecture, and graphic design that I wasn't able to include in this book. My hope is that the themes and designers examined serve as a starting point for readers to begin their own investigations into this part of the creative sector in order to foster more knowledge, develop some healthy scepticism, and ultimately help the ongoing move toward change.

A CHANGE IN FASHION

The implicit tension born out of the demand for Black creativity and the reality of white society's refusal to treat Black designers as equal to their white counterparts is an issue that persists today but was particularly acute in the years preceding the Civil Rights Act. For Ann Lowe, this meant being given the opportunity to design Jackie Kennedy's wedding dress in 1953 while being denied recognition for it when Kennedy referred to Lowe only as her "colored woman dressmaker" in an interview. In a similar way, American fashion and costume designer Zelda Wynn Valdes is often wrongly cited for designing the Playboy Bunny outfit. Her more interesting (and factually correct) claim to fame lies in the designer-and-muse relationship she formed with singer and actress Joyce Bryant. As costume designer for the famously all-black ballet company, Dance Theatre of Harlem, Valdes also played an important role in artistic resistance during the Civil Rights Movement.

A disregard for the work of Black designers leads to a complex issue of legacy. Daniel Day, known as Dapper Dan, ran into difficulty at the beginning of his career when he used the logos of luxury designers without their consent. However, in 2017, Gucci created a mink bomber jacket for their Resort 2018 show which resembled one designed by Dapper Dan in the early 1990s, which caused a social media furor resulting in what is now an ongoing collaboration between Dapper Dan and Gucci. This arc creates an uncomfortable question about why it took Gucci's endorsement of Dapper Dan to legitimize his designs when he had already been selling to prominent African Americans from the start.

One fashion designer who excelled with an ironic nod to Blackness was Patrick Kelly. In 1985, he sent a model down the runway with a golliwog cartoon printed on the front of a dress. He later adopted the golliwog logo with his name in bold letters around the blackface. He honed his aesthetic of bold colors and racial references when he moved to Paris. Once there, he dressed celebrities such as Grace Jones, Isabella Rossellini, and Madonna. What could be read as a success story starts to fall apart when you compare the fame and adulation bestowed upon Kelly's contemporaries and the care taken to preserve their legacies.

"A DISREGARD FOR THE WORK OF BLACK DESIGNERS LEADS TO A COMPLEX ISSUE OF LEGACY."

For example, Yves Saint Laurent has a museum in Paris and an ongoing business worth billions, while the innumerable books and documentaries on Coco Chanel are only matched by the endless homages paid to Christian Dior. And yet many people who would consider themselves interested in fashion have never heard of Patrick Kelly or examined the impact of his designs that reclaimed Black tropes as luxury items.

Where Kelly and Dapper Dan chaffed against the dominant conventions of their field, Willi Smith, hailed as the most commercially successful Black American designer of the twentieth century, enjoyed a warm reception from the white fashion world and the Black community alike. As he was embraced by the mainstream, he found he did not need to reference his Blackness in his work but instead sought to design clothes for "people on the streets" of every color.

In current times, Black designers are often faced with the challenge of navigating a fashion world that tends toward restrictive views of Black design. LaQuan Smith, New York–based creator of his flirtatious namesake womenswear line, has noted the tendency for the industry to box Black designers into a corner rife with stereotypes, while he pushes against the "urban" badge he never asked for. One response to sidestepping casual industry discrimination has been to ideate and produce on African soil. Kenneth Ize, a 2019 finalist of the LVMH Prize for Young Fashion Designers, creates hand-woven textiles for his label in a small factory that he owns and operates in Nigeria. Where many designers would have seen making the exclusive shortlist of the prize as a sign to move to the commercial fashion centers of London, Paris, or Milan, Ize has taken his acclaim and invested it in Lagos where he continues to create collections with brands like Karl Lagerfeld. Similarly,

Sindiso Khumalo, a South African native and recipient of the LVMH Prize in 2020, designs her own textiles and produces with local NGOs in South Africa and Burkina Faso.

Telfar Clemens, the queer, Liberian designer, has had incredible success by setting his label up in direct opposition to the exclusivity cultivated by luxury brands. With the mantra, "not for you, for everyone," Telfar has positioned high-end design as accessible with vocal commentary on the closed nature of the fashion industry. Clemens's work with the Liberian Olympic team—he designed and sponsored the kits for the Tokyo 2020 Olympic games—also reflects a wider trend where Black designers are encouraging a reassessment and education of the West's relationship with Africa by spotlighting their country of origin. Similarly, Bianca Saunders has created an aesthetic that is rooted in her experiences as a second-generation Jamaican in London.

REDEFINING ARCHITECTURE

In architecture, as in fashion, Black designers have been pushing against the confines of a Western society that refuses to look past the color of their skin. Paul Revere Williams, an architectural juggernaut who began his career in 1921, created luxury homes for Hollywood icons and yet, had to develop elaborate tactics in order to avoid uncomfortable situations with his patrons. The work of Norma Sklarek, who was the first African American woman member of the American Institute of Architects, is another case of "lost" identity. We are in a time where celebrating the historical and current achievements of women is a focus. My son is obsessed with the children's book series *Little People, Big Dreams*, where Amelia Earhart and Greta Thunberg feature alongside Black figures like Harriet Tubman, Josephine Baker, and Rosa Parks. But where there is acknowledgment for Zaha Hadid, Sklarek, who had a less visible career but did great things for Black people in architecture and designed buildings of note, is nearly forgotten.

Chicago-born architect Hilyard Robinson is an example of a Black designer whose practice is of huge significance and yet undervalued. Working as codesigners in the mid 1930s, Robinson and Paul Revere Williams were the lead architects of Langston Terrace Dwellings, the first federally funded housing project in Washington, DC, and one of the first four in the United States. The fact that Robinson's work is barely celebrated says something devastating about the ethos of "for us, by us": the first housing project designed by African American architects, constructed by African American laborers, and open to African American families is not an event of note.

Meanwhile, in Africa, architects were choosing to reject the Western tradition of architecture in favor of indigenous techniques and solutions for African buildings. The work of John Owusu Addo and Oluwole Olumuyiwa spoke to a more formal sense of freedom—both designers began working in Ghana and Nigeria respectively once the countries had become independent from colonial rule. The political regimes in the late 1990s called for a new era of locally led buildings but the formal, Western design education undertaken by Addo and Olumuyiwa meant that they were operating from the same model as the white architects that came before them. We are not in the early days of African independence anymore, and yet there is still a bias in design curriculums—and all educational curriculums—where techniques and styles developed by Black designers go ignored.

Thankfully, there is a new generation of designers circumventing colonial educations and using their practice to illuminate their cultural heritages, including Demas Nwoko, Joe Osae-Addo, and Diébédo Francis Kéré. Nwoko incorporates modern technologies with traditional African techniques to highlight his African roots in his designs. Joe Osae-Addo, the acclaimed African architect, is evangelical about centering Africa in his practice. His firm uses a system that brings together architecture, urban planning, building technology, and landscaping that is geared toward the creation of "inno-native" design solutions. Similarly, the practice of Burkina Faso–born architect Diébédo Francis Kéré openly points to Afro-futurism as the organizing principle for his work.

DESIGN AS SOCIAL COMMENTARY

Jackie Ormes, known as the first African American woman cartoonist, could have had a lot of fun illustrating the exclusion of Black architectural achievements and Black women from the public record. Her work on the *Chicago Defender* and *Pittsburgh Courier* during the 40s and 50s presented a nuanced, powerful image of Blackness. Conversely, fellow artist Charles Dawson appeared to have a different viewpoint on what constituted progress for Black lives. Although he did not think the abolition of segregation was essential to the prosperity of the Black community, he was deeply concerned with the predicament of African Americans and acted to elevate their position in society through the curation of the little-known American Negro Exposition held in Chicago in 1940. What I find essential about Dawson's viewpoint is the very fact that it differs from the expected Black discourse of the time while still showing commitment to the advancement of African Americans. In Dawson's divergence, we're reminded that there is no singular Black mindset.

Emory Douglas's involvement with the Black Panther Party was pivotal in his assertion that design should be a call to action and a means of overthrowing oppression. Art Sims and Emmett McBain both took paths that focused on Black designs for Black audiences. Sims's film posters were prolific in the 80s, and his signature hand was utilized for various Spike Lee films as well as Steven Spielberg's *The Color Purple*. Any stardust absent in the offerings of McBain is compensated for by his seminal ad in 1968, "Black is Beautiful." Common to the output of both designers is the choice to work on briefs where Black people are the stars of their own show. Being reliant on Black endorsements meant that both designers could, (and in Sims's case, continue) to design without a studied eye on the reaction of the white establishment. Their work creates an intimacy with their Black audience and a model for design rooted in freedom.

Today, a new generation of graphic designers are using their craft to satirize popular culture and the Black tropes that exist within it. Of particular note is the work of Liz Montague who is (probably) the first Black cartoonist for *The New Yorker*. Her work centralizes Black characters with a layer of humor that act as a knowing nod to the double frustrations of Black women in a society that is at turns sexist and racist.

To all of these designers, from Ann Lowe to Kenneth Ize, Jackie Ormes to Liz Montague, Paul Revere Williams to Diébédo Francis Kéré, and to the many that I have not been able to cover in this book who are doing meaningful, vital work, I feel a great debt. As seismic shifts have taken place in the world that have directly affected the experience of Blackness, their approach to their practice has suggested a way to navigate these realities. What their work and trajectories provide is a feeling of hope, the sense that things are moving, are becoming better, and that at some point Black people—designers or otherwise—might have the freedom and space to really be seen.

FASHION

INTRODUCTION

There is an intimacy at play when you wear the clothes of a fashion designer. The garment is badged with their name, and the silhouette and material point to the individual (or the fashion house) as the maker. Therefore, when you choose who to wear, you are communicating both a look and an alignment with the label that made it. Some people take this process very seriously and appreciate how their fashion choices can speak to their values and perspectives on the world. Others demonstrate less consideration, but whether you have contemplated your fashion for hours or made a snap decision, what you select says something about who you are, what you care about, and the society we live in.

Black fashion designers and their stature in the cultural landscape can act as a tracker for the dialogue taking place between white and Black society. When we look at the Black female designers Ann Lowe and Elizabeth Keckley, who contributed to the historical canon of First Lady fashion, we see that Black craft was often coveted, while the designers behind that craft were not. The discovery of Zelda Wynn Valdes as a polymath points to the surface-level attention that was (and often still is) paid to the work of Black female creatives. Dapper Dan, Patrick Kelly, and Willi Smith's relationship with Blackness and Black communities speaks to the complexities Black people can face in pursuing success within and outside of their own communities. The assessment of how value is bestowed upon and reclaimed by Black fashion designers walks through the trajectory of LaQuan Smith, asking what role social media plays in providing and limiting Black power, while in the work of Sindiso Khumalo and Kenneth Ize we question what it means for Black people to redefine what success is. Finally, the efforts made by Bianca Saunders and Telfar Clemens to bring the entirety of their Black experience to their work is reflective of a wider revolution of Black people escaping the confines of code-switching to celebrate their culture in their professions.

Together, these chapters survey a patchwork of progress made, obstacles negotiated, and barriers presented while Black fashion designers have sought to assert their identities and creative language in a space that has not readily afforded them the opportunity to do so. In viewing the trajectories of their careers, there is something to be learned about the boxes Blackness has been placed into within the architecture of creativity and the joyful outcomes that ensue when those structures begin to collapse.

FIRST LADIES

Since 1912, the First Lady has donated a dress, traditionally their inaugural gown, to represent her in the First Ladies Collection at the Smithsonian's National Museum of American History. What began as a casual handing over of the garment has evolved into a national media event; by the time Michelle Obama presented her ivory, one-shouldered, embroidered Jason Wu, as well as a red gown also designed by Wu for the second inauguration, the now formal presentations were covered in the *New York Post*, the *Hollywood Reporter*, *USA Today*, and a host of other outlets. Hysteria peeked when the Smithsonian unveiled the First Lady portrait by Amy Sherald with Obama, wearing a stretch cotton poplin dress with corset-style lacing by New York label Milly, perched on a chair. *The Washington Post* suggested that "The dress has caused a stir not simply because it will be enshrined in history but also because it has such a central place in such a nontraditional portrait." [1]

To investigate this "stir" brings us to a simple truth: the First Lady and the First Lady's clothes say something about what society should value. Michelle Obama is the First Lady. Message: Black people are not trash. Jason Wu is a New York–based designer who was born in Taiwan, raised in Vancouver, and regularly collaborated with RuPaul. Message: immigrants are Americans (yes, this needs to be relearned by some); American society should be inclusive. Milly, at the time co-owned by Michelle Smith and her husband, was designed and manufactured in New York with a price point that didn't widen the eyes. Message: American design is sophisticated and unburdened by class associations; female entrepreneurship is important. So what does it mean when former First Lady Jackie Kennedy, the benchmark for style and grace, refuses to name check the "colored dressmaker" who designed and

OPPOSITE: Michelle Obama wearing the white gown designed by Jason Wu for the inaugural ball, 2009.

A cream silk faille dress with embroidered
floral appliqué decorations designed by
Ann Lowe, 1958.

painstakingly produced the wedding dress she wore at her wedding to John F. Kennedy? What does it say when a white woman with the power to change the world of a Black female designer, uses that strength to vanquish her from history with a dismissive sigh?

St. Louis Post-Dispatch's Debra D. Bass wrote in 2009 that the American First Lady is an influential, national icon of style, fashion, and poise "because at any given moment, she is the snapshot of the American woman."[2] Bass clearly wasn't thinking about women of color when she wrote this but was instead pointing to the aspirations of a white female contingent. In a similar vein, when JFK came to power, Oleg Cassini, the designer behind Jackie Kennedy's inaugural gala gown and sometimes referred to as her "Secretary of Style," predicted that "[t]he Jackie Kennedy look will sweep the country."[3] And it did. Women went wild for her coat dresses, pill box hats, and elbow-length gloves. On a trip to Europe in 1961 as president, JFK famously joked that he was "the man who accompanied Jacqueline Kennedy to Paris."[4]

The appetite for obsessive details regarding Jackie Kennedy's clothes is well illustrated by the strange public spat that ensued between Kennedy and subsequent First Lady Pat Nixon. As newspapers closely followed Jackie's fashion choices, noting a penchant for Balenciaga and Chanel, estimates of her wardrobe budget were bandied about, fueling a bizarre, albeit mild-mannered slanging match between Nixon and Kennedy on who had spent more money on clothes. "I'm sure I spend less than Mrs. Nixon on clothes. She gets hers at Elizabeth Arden, and nothing there costs less than $200 or $300 [$2,021.42 and $3,032.12 in 2023]," Kennedy told the *New York Times* in 1960.[5] Nixon's response serves as a masterclass in cold restraint, as she did not "criticize other women—I've made it a practice not to." [6] Concerns over where Kennedy spent her dollars extended to US fashion designers, as a 1960 article in the *Baltimore Sun* reported that designers were "very confident that Kennedy would focus on primarily supporting the American fashion industry"[7] once she became First Lady. Jackie's history with Ann Lowe suggests that the collective confidence of US designers might have been seriously misplaced.

When I first started to read about Ann Lowe, it struck me that nearly every reference led with the fact that she designed Jackie Kennedy's dress. If it wasn't for this unlikely connection, it is unclear whether Lowe would have had—and subsequently held—the level of interest that this relationship had granted her. Therefore, to a large extent, the value of Lowe's designs and career have been defined by the famous white lady she dressed, and this fact, when taken as the headline of her life, reduces her to a supporting character in another person's legacy.

LEFT: Bridal portrait of Jackie Kennedy shows her in an Ann Lowe-designed wedding dress, 1953.

OPPOSITE: Ann Lowe's letter to Jackie Kennedy outlining her upset at being called a "colored woman dressmaker" in the *Ladies Home Journal*, April 5, 1961.

Lowe was commissioned to design Jacqueline Lee Bouvier's wedding dress in 1953. The piece, a silk taffeta number with a modest neckline and embroidered skirt, is sometimes referred to as the most photographed wedding dress in history. Lowe received the commission after years of working with the Bouvier family as their dressmaker. What should have been a glorious moment was overshadowed by an early disaster. Ten days before the wedding, a flood in Lowe's Manhattan studio ruined ten of fifteen gowns, including the wedding dress. After working around the clock to remake the gowns, Lowe ultimately lost $2,200 for the job. Rather than informing Kennedy and potentially recouping some of the money, Lowe absorbed the losses.

A 1966 interview with Lowe in *Ebony* magazine provides some insight: "I love my clothes and I'm particular about who wears them," Lowe said. "I am not interested in sewing for cafe society or social climbers. I do not cater to Mary and Sue. I sew for the families of the Social Register."[8] What comes across here is the pride that Lowe took from being a society dressmaker, a splash of snobbery, and an understanding of her worth. A *New Yorker* profile by Judith Thurman further attests to Lowe's pride, describing how "She did, however, indignantly refuse to use the service entrance at the Auchincloss farm, threatening to take her work back to New York if it and she weren't ushered through the front door."[9]

Taking these indications of pride as a window into Lowe's character, one can assume that Kennedy's subsequent snub would have been painful both professionally and personally. The idea that Lowe's feelings were hurt is evidenced in her robust response to the First Lady's

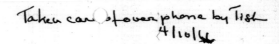

Taken car of over phone by Tish
4/10/6

Ann Lowe's Gowns

~~976 LEXINGTON AVENUE AT 71ST STREET~~
NEW YORK 21, N. Y.
~~TElephone 8-3333~~

5 April 1961

Dear Mrs. Kennedy;

My reason for writing this note is to tell you
how hurt I feel as a result of an article, the last
of a series, about you in the Ladies Home Journal in
which the reporter stated your wedding gown was by a
"colored woman dressmaker, not the haute couture." I
realise it was not intentional on your part but as you
once asked me not to release any publicity without your
approval, I assume that the article in question, and
others, was passed by you.

You know I have never sought publicity but I would
prefer to be referred to as a " noted negro designer,"
which in every sense I am. My name does not need to be
mentioned as many of my socially prominent customers
know I did your wedding as I have your wedding portrait
prominently displayed on my office wall.

Please try to have any reference to me correctly
stated as I have worked hard to achieve a certain position
in life which has been considerably more difficult due to
my race. At this late point in my career, any reference
to the contrary hurts me more deeply than I can perhaps
make you realise.

Thanking you for any consideration you might show
me and wishing you and your family well, I remain,

As ever;

Ann Lowe

ANN LOWE

refusal to admit her existence in a 1961 *Ladies' Home Journal* interview. According to the article, the gown had been made by "a colored woman dressmaker, not the haute couture."[10] Rather than take the silent route which would have been expected due to the racial power dynamics of the time, Lowe dispatched a letter to Kennedy: "My reason for writing this note is to tell you how hurt I feel. You know I have never sought publicity, but I would prefer to be referred to as a 'noted negro designer,' which in every sense I am . . . Any reference to the contrary hurts me more deeply than I can perhaps make you realize."[11] In an attempt to smooth things over, Letitia Baldridge, Kennedy's social secretary, called Lowe to offer an apology for her distress without admitting that the First Lady was the arbiter of that pain. Rather than placating Lowe, the conversation led to her seeking an attorney and ultimately demanding redress from the *Ladies' Home Journal*, which they, somewhat cruelly, denied her.

Tragedy is what pours out of this particular Ann Lowe story—the wet dresses discarded and redone, the Judas-like denial of her craft, the refusal by the *Ladies' Home Journal* to acknowledge the mistake. Yet, what I find to be the saddest part of all is what seems to be Lowe's fundamental misunderstanding of her relationship with these socialites, namely that she thought that these women saw her as she saw herself, "a noted negro designer,"[12] when in reality, their actions suggested that she was another form of hired help.

Even when you look at the dress of which she was so proud, fashion historians believe that it was never Jackie's first choice. "Even though it's a beautiful dress, it was not what she wanted, and she actually compared it to a lampshade," says fashion historian Kimberly Chrisman-Campbell. "It was chosen by her father-in-law-to-be, who wanted to create an American royalty moment and really set up his son as the heir to the family dynasty."[13] The unembarrassed haggling these society

Now You See Me

ladies engaged in when procuring Lowe's clothes also speaks to an imbalance in regard. "The same millionaires who cherished the finesse of her needlework haggled shamelessly over her prices," Thurman writes. "Retailers profited from her label's cachet but didn't advance the costs of her materials or her labor, and the debts she incurred to suppliers helped ruin her."[14]

Lowe's life story is now positioned as the discovery of a great designer. And she was great—the wedding dress, whether Jackie loved it or not, would have influenced a million dresses across the globe. Yet Lowe's experience is also an example of the boxes that Black designers were placed in at the time—mainly, out of sight. Lowe was "society's best-kept secret,"[15] but why was she a secret at all when these same ladies were squawking about their Balenciaga and YSL from their gilded balconies? Because the wearing of a Black designer was nothing to be proud of. Ann Lowe designs were not a sign of status but a form of guilty pleasure. This woman who would later be described by Jessica Regan, an associate curator at the Metropolitan Museum of Art's Costume Institute, as "a sculptural designer whose work was a dialogue with the body of the woman who wore it,"[16] bore a name whispered, rather than shouted. This was a mistake; Lowe's life and her achievements were extraordinary.

Lowe was born December 14, 1898, in Clayton, Alabama, to Janie and Jack Lowe. Her mother and grandmother ran a dressmaking business catering to political wives and daughters in the early 1900s. As Lowe got older, she would help her mother with the dresses. When Janie died in 1914, Lowe, sixteen at the time, was called upon to finish the ball gowns for Alabama's First Lady, Elizabeth Kirkman O'Neal. At this point Lowe was already married to Lee Cone, with whom she had a son. When a chance encounter in 1916 with Josephine Lee, the wife of a wealthy citrus grower, led to Lowe being offered a live-in job to make wedding gowns for Lee's twin daughters, Lowe left her husband in Montgomery and moved with her son to Tampa, Florida, beginning a lifelong entwinement with white high society.

It is not an original observation to note that money and power can be intoxicating and motivating. Lowe, the great granddaughter of an enslaved woman and an Alabama plantation owner, was clearly enamored by her proximity to wealth and status, and this may well have fueled her ambitious trajectory once she made it to Tampa. By 1920 she had her own store, Annie Cone, with eighteen dressmakers underneath her. During this time, she also spent a brief but successful stint at the reputable S. T. Taylor Design School in New York (it is said that she left after the French tutor felt that he had nothing left to teach her, but her departure may have had more to do the school's segregation policies). Meanwhile in Tampa, she developed a reputation as a Gasparilla gown aficionado for the city's annual Gasparilla Pirate Festival, a local event since 1904 that included balls for the city's wealthiest residents. Girls from the most prestigious families were elected to a Gasparilla court with one being crowned queen—it was like the Met Gala of Tampa except that everyone who was anyone wore a gown by Ann Lowe. "If you didn't have a Gasparilla gown by Annie, you might as well stay home," Alexandra Frye wrote in the *Tampa Tribune*. "The amazing element in all of this is that Ann Lowe never worked with a pattern. All the designs flow straight from her creative mind onto material."[17]

The open praise and support that Lowe received in Tampa was not reflective of the segregation issues rampant in Tampa at the time. Lowe was unable to rent a space in the downtown business district. Her clients had to visit her in a segregated space that she was able to procure. For someone so attuned to what is and isn't proper, this must have been humiliating. A 1927 Tampa business study suggested that "[i]nterracial contact between the white and colored elements in Tampa, as elsewhere in the South, [were] for the most part limited to those of a business nature."[18] There were only 185 Negro businesses in a population of 23,323 Negroes; of these businesses, two were dressmakers. The study further suggests that "Some people place the Negro business man in contest with the White business man and views his products from a standpoint of quality, price, quantity and service."[19] Though this was certainly the case with Lowe—in so far as hers was a product contest she had clearly won—she still made the decision to move to New York in 1928. Given the success of her business and open recognition as a great dressmaker, the move, along with the brief stint at S. T. Taylor Design School, creates a portrait of a woman who aspired to be "more." As a guest on the *Mike Douglas Show* in 1964, she described her driving ambition to prove that a Negro can become a "leading American dress designer."[20] New York, with its bright lights and moneyed society, was the place where Lowe would be seen.

Lowe's move to New York did not begin brilliantly. Lowe had married a hotel bellman named Caleb West, with whom she lived in Harlem with her son. At first, she rented out a studio where she worked with her assistants on gowns for an old Tampa client. Eventually, she began to make gowns on spec for upscale department stores such as Henri Bendel, Montaldo's, I. Magnin, Chez Sonia, Neiman Marcus, and Saks Fifth Avenue until she eventually met the "right people" and opened her own salon, Ann Lowe's Gowns, on Lexington Avenue. It was around this time in 1953 that she received the commission to make Jacqueline Lee Bouvier's wedding dress. This should have been a career defining moment worthy of much celebration. We know this wasn't the case. Instead, the latter half of the 50s and early 60s was personally and financially ruinous for Lowe.

Ann Lowe fitting a dress to a mannequin, 1966.

In 1958, her son Arthur Lee, who'd been instrumental in managing Lowe's finances, died in a car accident. The subsequent emotional and financial turmoil led to the closing of Lowe's salon in 1962 due to unpaid taxes. A year later, Lowe lost an eye to glaucoma. While she was in hospital, an unknown benefactor paid off her debts. Lowe believed it was Jackie Kennedy—whether she was right or wrong, the very fact that she still sought some sort of acknowledgement from Kennedy speaks volumes. Free of debt, she agreed to take on a role at Saks as the head designer of the Adam Room. Unfortunately, Lowe found herself making debutante and wedding gowns for elite clientele at an unsustainable cost—she had to pay for her supplies and fabric, as well as her staff, while Saks set the prices. As Lowe explained, "Too late, I realized that dresses I sold for $300 were costing me $450."[21] A prestigious collaboration that should have been a moment of triumph for Lowe instead became another burden she had to endure. As she later told the *New York Daily News*, she "almost gave up dreaming about beauty and thought only of suicide."[22]

Portrait of Elizabeth Keckley [date unknown].

It's clear that Lowe was a terrible businesswoman. In contemporary parlance, she needed to own that. It's also clear that the white people around her saw absolutely no moral or cognitive quandary in championing the aesthetic value of Lowe's work while systematically undermining her status as a designer and economic well-being. In an interview with *Ebony* in 1966, one of Lowe's clients stated, "Lowe dresses are worth more than they cost. They are works of art—timeless, feminine, beautiful, always the most flattering gown a woman could choose."[23] Is it just me, or does something that should be an apologetic admission of guilt read as a boast? The inclination to attach less economic value to the labor of Black people spreads far beyond Lowe and fashion design, with roots so deep in slavery, colonialism, and systemic racism that we still need trackers and government working groups to address the problem today. What is particular to the time and Lowe's situation is that no one seems confused about her talent: Olivia de Havilland was happy to wear an Ann Lowe gown to accept her Oscar for Best Actress in the film *To Each His Own* in 1947, but she removed the tag marking it as a Lowe dress before attending the ceremony; Jackie Kennedy (potentially under duress) wore a Lowe wedding dress and wouldn't admit it; Saks had a salon headed by Lowe but wouldn't pay her properly. What all these slights have in common is that they come with a kiss. The story goes that she was never recognized, that her talent was never given the due it deserved. What I see in Lowe's erasure is worse than that. Her talent was fully, clearly seen, but the white society around her—the people she held so dear and cared deeply about—simply did not believe she deserved anything in exchange for her talent—not money, not status, and definitely not respect.

Unbelievably, there is another Black seamstress born in the nineteenth century whose life is entangled with an ungrateful First Lady. Elizabeth Keckley was born into slavery in Virginia in 1818 as the daughter of Agnes Hobbs and Hobbs's owner, Colonel Armistead Burwell. Like Ann Lowe, Keckley learned how to sew from her mother. This skill, along with the ability to perform general house and childcare duties, led her first to North Carolina with Burwell's son and wife, then on to St. Louis, Missouri, with Burwell's daughter and her husband. An essential distinction here is that this movement across states occurred with Keckley as a slave—a fact brought into sharp focus by the fact that she was repeatedly raped by her next-door neighbor, Alexander Kirkland, while in North Carolina, which led to the birth of her son, George.

The brutality that Keckley suffered did not manifest outwardly. "[A] face strong with intellect and heart, with enough of beauty left to tell you that it was more beautiful still before wrong and grief had shadowed it"[24] is how she was described by Mary Clemmer Ames in an article

"WHAT THE FIRST LADY WEARS SAYS SOMETHING ABOUT WHAT SOCIETY SHOULD VALUE"

for *The Evening Post.* Historian Jennifer Fleischner described her as "striking to look at, independent-minded, and accomplished."[25] Keckley used her time in the new cities she found herself in to befriend white connections through her dress-making skills; in St. Louis, the charm offensive gained her patrons who together contributed $1,200 to allow Keckley to buy her and her son's freedom in 1855. By 1860, she had moved to Washington, where the same patrons who had facilitated her freedom introduced her to the socialite Mrs. Jefferson Davis, and ultimately to Mary Todd Lincoln, the First Lady.

Mary Todd Lincoln was no Jackie Kennedy when it came to influencing the style of the nation. But like Kennedy during the Civil Rights era, Lincoln began her relationship with Keckley during the Civil War era. Lincoln's family was from Kentucky, a border state where slavery was still permitted at the time, but she was a loyalist to her husband's policies and having a free Black dressmaker spoke to that loyalty.

The relationship between Lincoln and Keckley extended beyond the formal niceties of client and seamstress. It's understandable that Lincoln found solace in her friendship with Keckley. The South viewed the First Lady as a traitor for supporting the abolition of slavery, while many in the North regarded her as a spy; everyone else criticized her for her supposedly ostentatious purchases for the White House. The closeness of the two women goes some way to explaining why it came as such a shock to both society and Lincoln when fifty-year-old Keckley published a book in 1868 providing intimate details of her life in the White House. Ostensibly, Keckley wrote about her life with Lincoln to set the record straight about the First Lady, who she saw as being unfairly maligned; there was also the practical matter of making money. *Behind the Scenes: Or, Thirty Years a Slave, and Four Years in the White House* was remarkable for the fact that it existed as a first-person documentation of life as a Black female at the time. What she spoke of was extraordinary in the unflinching assessment she gave of the First Lady. "It may be charged that I have written too freely on some questions, especially in regard to Mrs. Lincoln. I do not think so."[26] Her text caused shockwaves in Washington society with its exhaustive and sometimes blistering take on Mary Todd Lincoln's moods and her unsuccessful and embarrassing quest to sell her wardrobe after Abraham Lincoln's assassination. Though Lincoln was furious, and Keckley's other high-society clients, fearful that their lives too would be laid bare, stopped wearing her designs, she was unrepentant. "[W]hy should I not be permitted to lay her secret history bare," she wrote, "especially when that history plainly shows that her life, like all lives, has it's good side as well as its bad side?"[27]

In 1885, having stopped working as a dressmaker, Keckley helped to establish the National Home for Destitute Colored Women and Children, where she later died in 1907. If you compare the sacrifice of her career with Lowe's almost ceaseless deference—punctuated with the odd show of defiance—for high-society right until the end, Keckley's journey, from slave to the heart of power at the White House, provides a clear-eyed view of what it took to survive and prosper at a time when neither outcome was guaranteed. In the case of both women, their status was ultimately linked to their relationship with the First Lady, but neither crumbled entirely when that patronage was ripped away from them. The strong Black woman has become a trope played out against an "I Will Survive" soundtrack, but the temerity and resilience displayed by Lowe and Keckley is gratifying to witness.

I began by saying that what the First Lady wears says something about what society should value, and this is true of the attire of all those in power—they send visual signals to the rest of the world, through design, and most visibly, through fashion, about what and who is and is not important. Michelle Obama's purposeful use of fashion provides a glowing example of the positive influence on the industry, while the example of Ann Lowe demonstrates the devastating affect that clandestine patronage can have on the precarious life of a Black designer. Perhaps we have the most to learn from the actions of Keckley, who used her proximity to the First Lady to communicate her own story without filter. There was triumph in Keckley's designs and in her ascent to being Lincoln's primary dressmaker for seven years, and even more to be admired in how she risked it all to use her voice and her position as a designer to stand alone in her truth. "Notwithstanding all the wrongs that slavery heaped upon me, I can bless it for one thing—youth's important lesson of self-reliance."[28] And what better lesson is there for Black designers, constantly enthralled to gatekeepers, than that?

ZELDA WYNN VALDES: A BLACK POLYMATH

A jack of all trades, master of none, is not a real thing.

Author of *The Polymath* Waqas Ahmed states, "Polymathy is the optimal path to creativity because, by its very nature, it requires you to be diverse in your experience and your learning."[29] The *Oxford English Dictionary* defines a polymath as "A person of much or varied learning; one acquainted with various subjects of study," but Ahmed is referring strictly to those who have made "significant contributions" to a minimum of three fields, for example, Leonardo da Vinci (artist, inventor, and anatomist). The average person flings the term around loosely to mean anyone who actively pursues more than one discipline with recognition and acceptance from experts in their respective fields.

Though self-proclaimed industry experts across all fields are overwhelmingly male and overwhelmingly white, there are noted historical Black polymaths such as W.E.B. Du Bois, a sociologist, historian, philosopher, fiction writer, and editor. One could also point to Africanus Horton, a nineteenth-century medical doctor, banker, scientist, and political thinker who was an early advocate of African Nationalism. The Black design polymath in recent history has mostly appeared as a Black musician. An early template for these endeavors was created by P. Diddy with his Sean Combs fashion label, which was awarded the CFDA Fashion Award for the Menswear Designer of the Year in 2004. Jay Z and Damon Dash entered a similar arena with the multi-million grossing Rocawear. Though these brands had tremendous financial

OPPOSITE: Zelda Wynn Valdes fitting a dress to a mannequin [date unknown].

A black beaded full-length gown designed by Zelda Wynn Valdes and worn by Ella Fitzgerald, late 1940s.

success and some industry recognition, they were both pigeonholed as streetwear. As explained by *Guardian* fashion editor Priya Elan, most people think of that category as "Low-priced, soft-to-the-touch comfy wear that nods to hip-hop. They don't think of haute couture."[30] In recent years, there has been some evolution in this Black musician/ fashion designer dynamic. One change is that streetwear has firmly penetrated the luxury market, resulting in less snobbery around labels and designers that focus on the category. At the same time, it feels as if Black musicians have been able to explore design outside of streetwear, as with Frank Ocean's Homer brand of lab-grown diamonds or Swizz Beatz's design contribution to the Aston Martin Rapide.

But today, it's the very visible enterprise embodied by Virgil Abloh that signifies the Black polymath. It's almost impossible to use the term without imagining Abloh's head-spinning turns as DJ, architect, fashion designer, furniture designer, car designer, graphic designer, accessories designer, and interior designer. Though I may have accidentally left a few of Abloh's endeavors out, in the same way his friend and colleague Kanye West created a whole new environment for reflective hip-hop, Abloh, with a series of media-worshiped collaborations and products, propelled the Black design polymath into public consciousness, paving the way for a wave of polymaths to follow in his wake. Notably, Abloh's polymath network is largely dominated by Black men: Kanye West and the web that is Yeezy; Samuel Ross, founder of fashion label A-COLD-WALL and design studio SR_A, which encompasses luxury industrial design, interior installation, architecture, furniture design, sound design, and sculptural/visual communication; Tremaine Emory, founder of the label Denim Tears, creative director at Supreme, and cofounder of the creative incubator No Vacancy Inn.

It is not to say that there aren't successful Black women operating in multiple fields. Beyoncé has Ivy Park; Solange's creative collective Saint Heron produce everything from furniture to ceramics; and Rihanna founded Fenty Beauty and Savage X Fenty underwear, and was the first Black woman to have a (now defunct) fashion label with LVMH. The difference between the female examples that I've given and the male examples is that the women are still mostly recognized for their musical talent over their design achievements. One reason for this disparity might stem from the gendered application of the "artistic genius" badge which acts as close cousin of the polymath, and is an accolade rarely bestowed upon women, let alone Black women.

The road to, and motivation behind, multidisciplinary success has been thoroughly analyzed by academic researchers because "the world's problems require a multidisciplinary skillset—that is, the combination and involvement of several academic disciplines or professional specializations to a topic or problem."[31] More broadly, it's the idea that polymaths, with their unique perspective and ability to make connections, can create and develop ideas that are all together more interesting. In her PhD paper "In Pursuit of Polymaths: Understanding Renaissance Persons of the 21st Century," Angela Cotellessa investigated the experience of self-identifying modern polymaths and found that emotional robustness was required to pursue multiple interests. "Because we live in a society that tells us to specialize, and these are people who didn't do that—they forged their own path."[32] Of several conclusions from her dissertation, two stood out when I considered the importance of the Black female polymath in design, historically and today. The first is that "polymath identity is discovered from not fitting in; polymath identity can be difficult to fully own and to explain to others;"[33] and the second is that "family and financial resources impact the emergence of polymathy."[34]

There is no ticker that charts the number of self-identifying polymaths in the world, but we can deduce from Cotellessa's work that being Black and female might be the perfect and worst breeding ground for a design polymath. Perfect in that the intersection of being Black and female in an industry that is predominantly white and male should encourage a polymath identity in so far as fitting in as a Black woman in these spaces is hard; worst in relation to financial resources—the London School of Economics found that "Black women are the least likely to be among the UK's top earners compared to any other racial or gender group."[35] Though it's important to look at how self-identifying as a polymath might emerge, there is also tremendous social prestige in being labeled a polymath. To give Black female designers this label in full public glory helps to raise the value attached to their work. It suggests, wrongly or rightly, a certain intellectual and cultural acumen. Therefore, when I discovered the true breadth of activity from Zelda Wynn Valdes, it felt necessary to reassess her practice with that fact in mind: Zelda Wynn Valdes was a polymath. If we remember her as such, it might help us lavish the term more frequently on Black female designers today.

INTRODUCING ZELDA WYNN VALDES

While listening to the oral history of Zelda Wynn Valdes, I had to pause and wonder why I couldn't really remember what day of the week it was while she could recall details of events that had happened seventy years earlier. Those memories spanned her move to New York from Pennsylvania, her work as a seamstress, teaching piano, costume design at Dance Theatre of Harlem, the fashion shows she produced, and the dressing of some of the most famous musicians of the time. All of it was fascinating. And yet, the one "fact" that people know about Zelda Wynn Valdes is that she designed the iconic Playboy Bunny outfits, which, in fact, is untrue.

Valdes was born in Chambersburg, Pennsylvania, in 1905 as Zelda Christian Barbour, one of seven siblings. She often spoke about her grandmother and great grandmother's journey on the Underground Railroad and how they taught her to sew. Chambersburg was a very white town—she was the only Black person out of 135 to graduate from her high school—but one where she wasn't aware of suffering from any explicit racist antics. In her spare time, Valdes taught piano, and on the weekends she would pour over the *New York Times* and dream about moving to the city. So when the opportunity arrived to work with her uncle in White Plains, New York, she jumped at it. She was seventeen.

The timeless vision of New York as the place where big dreams are made played out as truth for Valdes. Starting as a seamstress at her uncle's tailoring store, she soon met the wife of the creator of Hellmann's mayonnaise, who asked Valdes to help her with her house decorations. For the next ten years, Valdes balanced work in interior design with her job at her uncle's store, finally going into a business on her own in White Plains as a seamstress during the Great Depression. By focusing on amendments while everyone was too stretched to buy new dresses, her shop thrived, and by the 40s, Valdes was producing fashion shows to showcase her designs. Her growing success in White Plains spread to her own boutique, Zelda Wynn, on West 158th Street and Broadway, which Valdes boasted was "the first black business on Broadway. All of Broadway—from Albany to the end of New York City."[36] That pride was expressed in beautiful window displays and a growing clientele of Black entertainers and elites for whom she designed dresses that accentuated their hourglass figures.

Joyce Bryant wearing one of the "tight-tight" gowns designed for her by Zelda Wynn Valdes, 1953.

Zelda Wynn Valdes at Dance Theatre of Harlem
where she designed many of the costumes for
the dancers [date unknown].

Zelda Wynn Valdes fitting a dress to Eartha Kitt, 1952.

Valdez's popularity peaked during the 40s and 50s. Her star-studded list of clients included Ella Fitzgerald, Dorothy Dandridge, Josephine Baker, Eartha Kitt, Mae West, and Marlene Dietrich. Not only did she attend the wedding of Maria Hawkins Ellington and Nat King Cole, she watched the bridal party shimmy around in her designs. She sold dresses for $800 ($9,400 today) that featured solid gold, diamond, and jewel trimmings. Louis Armstrong ordered four dresses for his vocalist Velma Middleton at a cost of $4,250 ($50,000 today). She talked popular singer Joyce Bryant into exploiting her shape with "a more aggressively sexy look, with 'tight, tight' gowns."[37] And Valdes flaunted her success. "The snappy convertible auto that Zelda Wynn, who designs Joyce Bryant's gowns, rides around in is a gift from her hubby Oscar. She plans to have a midget sewing machine built into the glove compartment."[38] And in 1949 she became a founding member of the National Association of Fashion and Accessory Designers (NAFAD) to help Black fashion creatives gain access to networking, professional development, and mentoring.

Before moving on to the next chapter of Valdes's achievements, it would serve us well to pause here and consider what she was building. The gowns she made celebrated the Black female form in a way that elevated careers. Her "snappy convertible" and fabulously expensive creations were seemingly so ostentatious that they were deemed media worthy. Her Broadway boutique was an emblem of Blackness on a predominately white street. By founding the NAFAD, where she was president of the New York chapter for several years, she formally recognized the importance of nurturing those who came after her. These are all achievements that individually would be impressive, but this endless switching from entrepreneur to activist to media celebrity to designer shows the mind of someone who understood early and accurately how different worlds could interact to bring success that went beyond individual goals. Valdes's sprawling repertoire helped to normalize the visual of Black extravagance while she supported others in navigating the system.

The second act of Valdes's life was in dance. The story goes that Arthur Mitchell, the director and choreographer of Dance Theatre of Harlem (DTH), would call Valdes's shop every day with zero luck until eventually his friend Lorenzo James caught up with her while she was hosting a dinner. After telling her about Mitchell, who had made history as the first Black principal dancer at New York City Ballet in 1955, she received a call from him later that night. "I have a ballet company," he said. "They are in dire need of costumes, and I understand you can make anything."[39]

OPPOSITE: Joyce Bryant in a figure-hugging gown by Zelda Wynn Valdes, 1953.

LEFT: Zelda Wynn Valdes fits a costume to dancer Yvonne Hall at Dance Theatre of Harlem [date unknown].

RIGHT: Mae West wearing a gown designed by Zelda Wynn Valdes, c. 1930.

OPPOSITE: Zelda Wynn Valdes dress label in a black beaded dress worn by Ella Fitzgerald, late 1940s.

Valdes was working on several different projects at the time. One was the Poverty Program, where she would go out to community centers and teach young women how to sew. She was also scouting for models and producing fashion shows at church. This was when the myth of Valdes as designer of the Playboy Bunny costume emerged. It may seem pedantic, but Valdes made the costumes rather than designed them. The actual idea for the outfits came from Bunny's Tavern, a bar Hefner would go to while he was at college. Zelda was then recommended as a seamstress to bring this idea to life. What's essential to this story is not really where the creative intellectual property lies, but in the misinformation and/or lack of curiosity about the detail. In the previous chapter when discussing Ann Lowe, we saw a hawkish appetite to remove the credit she deserved. With Valdes we see a similarly destructive urge to reduce the achievements and barriers that she smashed through into a neat tidbit about a commission to make an outfit that Hefner was nostalgic for. Both tactics achieve the same end: erasing the true extent of Valdes's and Lowe's accomplishments.

Valdes was sixty-five when she joined DTH in 1970; she continued working with them until 1995. Set up by Mitchell in 1969, the goal of DTH was to provide opportunities for local children and challenge stereotypes of what was "normal" in the classical realm. For the company's European debut at the Spoleto Festival in Italy in 1971, Valdes designed the costumes for the "Holberg Suite," Mitchell's first ballet. In the upcoming years, she made costumes for over eighty-two productions and instigated the very necessary (and now ubiquitous) trend of matching tights to the different skin tones of the dancers. The ongoing impact of DTH lies not only on the fertile ground it created as host to generations of Black dance talent, but also the legacy it has held for Wynn in the archives of costume that rest at the company.

Any one of Valdes's varied accomplishments is noteworthy, but together they form an example of extraordinary creative dexterity that deserves celebration. In an alternative, fairer reality, Valdes would be enjoying the same enthusiastic reappraisal as the white actress Hedy Lamarr, who in 2017 had a widely distributed feature documentary unearthing

"WHILE VALDES SET A PRECEDENT FOR BLACK FEMALE POLYMATHS, REAL RECOGNITION IS STILL HARD TO COME BY."

the significant contributions Lamarr had made to the field of science. Both Lamarr and Valdes were victims of the explicit misogynistic culture that pervaded the 30s and 40s, but the difference is that Lamarr is now getting her flowers in a global cinematic roll out. And though it may be better to be memorialized incorrectly rather than to not be remembered at all, this misremembering reflects the thinness of intentions to commemorate Black women and the simple lack of respect for our lived experiences.

While Valdes set a precedent for Black female polymaths, real recognition is still hard to come by. Consider again Rihanna, a musician, an activist, CEO, and founder of Fenty Beauty and Savage X Fenty underwear. Rihanna is a designer who has on more than one occasion seen a problem, such as the lack of skin color and shape diversity in underwear—and solved it, yet what many people are most interested in is her next album. "Rihanna hints her long-awaited next album will be 'completely different to how she wanted before'—after the singer cracked Forbes' Billionaires List"[40] headlined a *Daily Mail* article, rather than leading with the fact that her lingerie and beauty business was growing at a rapid rate. "Savor Rihanna's Fenty Ketchup—Because New Music May Still Take A While"[41] was the slightly mocking tone taken by *Bustle*, a media platform for young women. The mental elasticity required to appreciate her many talents seems to elude much of the press, leaving

Playboy Bunny costume made, but not designed,
by Zelda Wynn Valdes, 1962.

the recognition of her business savvy to her fanbase who have watched
and admired her meteoric rise as an entrepreneur. Compare this to a
Kanye or a Virgil, two Black men who have used their design talent to
disrupt spaces from furniture to album covers to high street fashion. In
Kanye's case, public opinion might be split on whether we'd prefer him
to keep making albums or concentrate on the performance art piece
that is his life, but his design talent is mostly undisputed. For Virgil, in
his life and his death, his genius was recognized. This is because even
within the sparse space of the recognized Black polymath, gender bias
and sexism occurs—being labeled a polymath and the particular type
of genius that bestows upon a designer is typically reserved for men.
The world is not invested in the success of Black women.

As with other Black women, famous and otherwise, Valdes was able
to achieve great success across a variety of fields, but the prevailing
system has not evolved into one where Black women are supported
in singular or multiple pursuits. We receive 0.34% of VC funding,[42] we
make up 1.2% of CEOs on the Fortune 500, [43] and yet we are more likely
to start a business than white men.[44] We should pay attention to this.
And when we look at Zelda Wynn Valdes, we should pay attention to
all of the work she did to set a benchmark for what Black women can
achieve. And we should thank her for it.

Maria Hawkins Ellington wearing a dress
designed by Zelda Wynn Valdes at her wedding
to Nat King Cole, 1948.

Nat King Cole and Maria Hawkins Ellington
wedding party with dresses designed by Zelda
Wynn Valdes, 1948.

BLACK LEGACY

MAINSTREAM (ADJECTIVE)

: THE IDEAS AND OPINIONS THAT ARE THOUGHT TO BE NORMAL BECAUSE THEY ARE SHARED
BY MOST PEOPLE; THE PEOPLE WHOSE IDEAS AND OPINIONS ARE MOST ACCEPTED[45]

In October 2020, *Forbes* announced that it would no longer be referring
to people of color as minorities. Mr. Rashaad Lambert, their director of
culture & community and founder of *For(bes) The Culture*, succinctly
and robustly explained that non-whites are already a global majority,
echoing the late singer Prince by repeating "there is nothing minor
about us."[46] This historic tendency to push Black people to the edges
has its fingerprints all over our language of success, with words like
"mainstream" and "popular culture" being used when deciding whether
or not someone has ascended to stardom, while terms such as "Ghetto
Superstar" are reserved only for a Black person who is famous in Black
circles (when white creatives are famous in smaller circles they are
mostly referred to as "Indie Darlings").

The thing about the *mainstream* or the environment "of the people
whose ideas and opinions are most accepted" is that this space is white.
When we ask if something or someone is successful, we are mainly
asking if the white world has accepted them. This question, though
loaded and compromised by a legacy of racism, is still an important
one: white people hold the majority of the world's wealth and with it
access to resources and contacts designers want and need to prac-

OPPOSITE: Rapper Roxanne Shante in a custom
Dapper Dan design using the Louis Vuitton
logo, c. 1989.

tice and broaden their craft. Yet this should not reduce the relevance or the weight of the Black gaze when assessing the journey of Black designers. We can ask whether the Black designers sought the approval of their community and what that said about their own relationship with Blackness. We can understand why a Black designer may have been cold-shouldered. We can even look at the current parameters for critiquing Black designers in a moment when even constructive criticism may be deemed as counterproductive to progress. Each investigative question allows us to consider the success and visibility of the fashion designers in this book not just in the mainstream, but within the Black community.

Grace Jones wearing a black leather jacket and Eiffel Tower hat designed by Patrick Kelly, 1989.

Now You See Me

HREE BLACK KINGS

pper Dan
RN AUGUST 8, 1944, HARLEM, NEW YORK
ACK, MALE FASHION DESIGNER

lli Smith
RN FEBRUARY 29, 1948, PHILADELPHIA, PENNSYLVANIA
ACK, MALE FASHION DESIGNER
D APRIL 17, 1987

trick Kelly
RN SEPTEMBER 24, 1954, VICKSBURG, MISSISSIPPI
ACK, MALE FASHION DESIGNER
D JANUARY 1, 1990

Portrait of Dapper Dan, 2018.

The Gap is the all-American, high street brand we haven't been able to get away from since 1969, when they sought to make denim jeans, hoodies, and white T-shirts the epitome of cool. Even with the closure of their European stores, it's hard to think of a brand more ubiquitous and mainstream. Although in recent years they have sought to blend their brand with designers who hold an outlier status—first with their ill-fated collaboration with fashion label Telfar, then a recently ended ten-year deal with Yeezy—they are essentially catering to a populist consumer. So it was a surprise when in early 2022, the Gap brand that had customarily been emblazoned across hoodies of various colors was ceremoniously replaced with a gargantuan marketing campaign consisting of billboards, NFTs, and famous faces introducing the new "DAP" hoodie, a collaboration with Dapper Dan.

The Gap is not Dapper Dan's first ride at the rodeo. His international star first rose in 2017 when a jacket he made for the Olympic track star Diane Dixon in 1989 was used in a Gucci show. Born Daniel Day in Harlem to Lily and Robert Day, Dapper Dan spent a short stint in prison before writing on Pan-Africanism for the Harlem newspaper *Forty Acres and a Mule*. In 1982, he went on to set up Dapper Dan's Boutique in Harlem, where the Dixon jacket was one of the many logo-heavy products he created. At first mirroring the hours of a bodega, the 24-hour store sold furs and then moved into monogrammed items that he printed himself with Louis Vuitton, Gucci, and MCM logos. Beloved by rappers LL Cool J and Run DMC as well as athletes like Mike Tyson and others, his designs became synonymous with a certain "swagalicious" attitude. His work did not go unnoticed by police who frequently raided the store. Brands were equally ferocious in their attempts to shut Dapper Dan's boutique down with Fendi finally succeeding in 1992 by winning a trademark infringement case.

When the Dixon piece reappeared on the runway, the Black response on Twitter was fierce, stunned by the hypocrisy of luxury brands previously shutting down the boutique now profiting from the very items they denounced. Gucci responded by labeling the appearance a "homage" and inviting Dapper Dan to design a collection with the house. The headlines that followed were all from a resurrection playbook: "Gucci Resurrects an 'Underground' Man"[47] ran *The New York Times* piece. "Dapper Dan Used to Knock Off Gucci. Now, He's Collaborating With Them,"[48] was the lead in the *Wall Street Journal*. The assumption in most of the stories was that by partnering with Gucci, Dapper Dan had

Dapper Dan standing outside his boutique in
Harlem [date unknown].

been legitimized as a designer, when he had in fact already established
himself as a force in the design world.

A statement made by Babak Radboy, creative director at Telfar, about
the "not to be" collab with the Gap provides an alternative perspective
to the heroing of Black designers and bigger brand collaborations. "We
grew up looking at the edifice of the mall and wanting to be part of it,
to have power there," he said. "Now we have realized we shouldn't. It
has been part of our survival to become content for a bigger brand so
they can make a statement about their racial solidarity. But the real
problem is the initial situation that blocks a designer's progress so
they need to say 'yes' to such a thing."[49] Whether or not one agrees
with Radboy's perspective on such collaborations, his argument is
interesting as it provides texture to what is otherwise a linear argument
for brand partnerships that ignores the perspective and experience of
marginalized communities. Maybe the headline for Dapper Dan is not
redemption by Gucci but redemption in his own community?

Of the time when his designs were mostly purchased by hip-hop stars,
athletes, and "hustlers," Day is quick to assert in a *New York Times*
interview that Black middle-class people laughed at his designs.

> "The years that I was in the underground, [after the store closed
> and before Gucci 'resurrected' his designs] you don't see no
> black publication talking about me. Think about all the great
> minds that had to leave Harlem because they weren't recognized
> here. It wasn't till the fashion industry recognized me that my
> community began to also... Middle-class blacks didn't buy. They

snubbed me. I remember in Morningside Park, we had the biggest block party in the city, period. Everybody from everywhere came. And I was walking by and heard someone on the microphone say, 'Dapper Dan with that fake Gucci'—like I was a laughing stock. It was humiliating. A lot of people didn't understand what I was doing. But today, they get it."[50]

I'm not sure what Dapper Dan's private thoughts are on exactly why people get it today, but it's not a simple process to unpack the endorsement from Gucci and the act of the Black community opening its arms. Consider that Dapper Dan's renaissance was very much led by the outcry on Black Twitter, but before this noise, there's scant evidence of a massive movement to resurrect his designs. And for a lot of people— Black and otherwise—the controversy with Gucci was the first time that they were actively aware of who Dapper Dan was, again suggesting that his rise has not been a grassroots movement in the Black community. There is also the historical issue of requiring the approval of the white elite in order for a Black brand or person to be seen as legitimate. It's less a matter of Black people jumping on the bandwagon but more of a long history of value extraction and imbalanced power dynamics that have led many of us to turn to a white elite for what is and isn't legitimate. The idea I love most, and the one that gives me the most hope, is that the Black community embraced Dapper Dan because the Black community is in a place where we feel safer and more willing to embrace ourselves.

Dapper Dan's Gucci billoard in Harlem advertising "made-to-order garments for your taste and specific measurements," 2018.

WILLI SMITH

Willi Smith, West Village, New York City, 1982.

Willi Smith, considered to be the most commercially successful Black American designer of the twentieth century and a pioneer of "street couture," had a complicated relationship with the Black community similar to Dapper Dan. While mostly adored, there was also criticism regarding his perceived lack of engagement with Black issues. In a 1984 profile by Lynn Darling in *Esquire*, Smith recalls a meeting with James Baldwin in the South of France, in which Baldwin was angry about the way America had treated him.

> "And so I said, 'If you're so angry, why don't you go back home, because that kind of anger over that long a time is not going to help the young people of today.' And I'm telling myself, 'Willi, you better pinch yourself again, you're supposed to be angry and you're not.' He did make me think I didn't take the world seriously enough. But I just don't have time to do everything."[51]

There is a familiar Groundhog Day quality to this exchange in that we can very much imagine this scene taking place between two Black creatives today. Perhaps an activist still very much a part of the grassroots and someone else who sees progress as transcending identity. I paused recently when reading an interview by the comedian and entrepreneur Mohamed Kheir on his strategic approach to managing fellow comedian Elsa Majimbo and her book partnership with Valentino: "we adjust 'Kenyan comedian' to 'comedian.' And we adjust 'first female Kenyan comedian to get a couture collaboration,' to 'first comedian to get a couture collaboration.' There is often times power and scale in simplicity."[52] He points out that no one knows where Timothée Chalamet is from. In Smith's description of his Baldwin meeting, he seems to adopt both Baldwin's righteousness and Majimbo's exasperation. When Smith recognizes the need to "pinch" himself, he acknowledges that there is much anger to be found in being Black. And yet, just as quickly, the excuse of not having "time to do everything" reduces that anger to a secondary concern, with his primary preoccupation being to make beautiful clothes.

An early talent, Smith began his first job as an illustrator for dress shop Prudence and Strickler at the age of fifteen in Philadelphia, where he was born Willi Donnell Smith on February 29, 1948. A double scholarship at New York City's Parsons School of Design came to pass after completing an internship with the couturier Arnold Scaasi. The director of admissions at the time, David C. Levy, recalls his assistant Carmela

Hedger Lembo, being astounded by Smith's talent. "I remember this very well, because she was so flabbergasted by the quality of his work that she burst into my office after he left to tell me about it and him. She believed he was the most talented fashion-design applicant she had ever seen."[53]

This early acceptance by the white design community was paralleled with enthusiastic admiration from Black people. Discussing the 2020 exhibition *Willi Smith: Street Couture* at Cooper Hewitt, Smithsonian Design Museum in New York, his friend Kim Hastreiter noted that Smith was adored by Black women in particular. "[For black women he became] their dream husband, dream boss, dream best friend, dream leader, their dream son, dream teacher. He represented so many dreams, their dreams for the future of their African American community."[54] The root of this reverence was the belief that he confounded negative perceptions of Black men with his unimpeachable talent and impeccable manners. Unlike Dapper Dan's early years, this respect was echoed by the fashion industry who bestowed Smith with the American Fashion Critics' Award for Women's Fashion in 1983, six years after he had started his label with friend Laurie Mallet, and eighteen years after studying design at Parsons. Smith further cemented his creative reputation by seeking collaborations outside the fashion world with artists Keith Haring, Christo, Dan Friedman, and Nam June Paik, including the costume work he did for Spike Lee's *School Daze*. In another famous battle between chicken and egg, it's unclear whether Smith's ingenuity and freedom in his collaborations were the result of a wider acceptance by the establishment or if these very acts endeared him to the industry. What is true is that he did not face the typical boxing in of most Black designers where he was expected to create in a way that fit the world's narrow idea of what Black culture was. It has become almost orthodox for Black creatives to reference their culture in both the making and discussion of their work, and for those where this is a true and organic evolution of their discipline, these nods are welcome. Smith's journey, with its suggestion of creative freedom, should remind us to be cognizant of the subtle pressures that Black designers have come under to lead with Blackness in their work.

The universal appeal was deliberate. "I don't design clothes for the Queen, but for the people who wave at her as she goes by"[55] is how the famous Smith quote goes. He was interested in comfortable garments

Willi Smith with his sister and model
Toukie Smith, 1980s.

Postcard, WilliWear 5th Avenue Store, c. 1987. Designed by M&Co (New York, New York, USA, 1979-1992), for WilliWear Ltd. (New York, New York, USA, 1976-1990). Offset lithograph on paper. 10 x 15.2 cm (6 x 4 in).

of the Issey Miyake school—one of the first big successes was a pair of cargo pants with an adjustable wraparound waistband that came in one size. "I'm trying to strip my clothes of nostalgia, of age, of everything that isn't practical,"[56] Smith explained to a journalist at *Women's Wear Daily*. "I'm not imposing any fantasy on anyone ... What's the point if you can't put the clothes anywhere in this world? Clothing should go hand in hand with society." The egalitarian approach to design co-existed with a pursuit of the avant-garde. In 1982, Smith presented the installation *Art as Damaged Goods* at what was then Project Space One (PS1), laying out white plaster clothes marked as evidence. Visitors were not allowed into the room and were instead forced to peer in while holding colored cards to their face. The same level of experimentation informed the work he would do in the Black space. His Alvin Ailey collaborations with choreographer Dianne McIntyre on "The Lost Sun" (1973) and "Deep South Suite" (1976) and his experimental film *Expedition*, a WilliWear spring 1986 collection presentation shot in Dakur, Senegal, in 1985 with a local cast, can be seen as a direct attempt by Smith to correct what he saw as the perception that his education and worldview made him "so white" when the success of these projects demonstrated a symbiosis between Smith and his Blackness.

If Smith's position or actions rattled the Black people around him, it's hard to find evidence of this. Instead, the conflict presents as more of an internal one. In the aforementioned *Esquire* piece, Smith provided his take on the fashion landscape in the late 60s and what he called "black designer hype." "The black look was in," he said. "Now, I'm a designer, I'm a creative person, and I'm black. All of a sudden I am getting pressure to be more black. What am I supposed to be? I have enough trouble relating to the contradictions of being a person, never mind being a black. I've always been this color. I'd get really annoyed when people would say I'm so white."[57] His source of irritation: "The system in the whole world is based on education and class structure and seeing the world. If you've done these things, that's what makes you white."[58] Smith's position is a sympathetic one for all of us who regularly suffer from the existential demands of simply existing, and it's also a very contemporary issue for the Black designer in an era when the shadow of Black Lives Matter is cast upon every profile or think piece relating to a Black creative. With this focus is a presumed affinity with Blackness that doesn't leave huge amounts of space for other elements that might inform one's identity or one's designs; or space for crisis and conflict outside of race that may rest in all the trouble of "being a person" that Smith alluded to. But the more illuminating argument is what he said about the system and how participation in the system "makes you white." The assumption here is that education, class, and exploring the world are the domain of whiteness—as Black people, that's definitely what we have been told. The irritation that Smith displayed for why those spaces are seen as "so white" would have been better channeled trying to explore why fundamental facets of our world are seen as non-Black environments.

PATRICK KELLY

Patrick Kelly wearing his golliwog logo, 1988.

Patrick Kelly's work also provokes uncomfortable questions. At times he faced "pushback" from the Black community who were perturbed by his use of Black iconography in his designs with golliwogs and watermelon motifs. "I get a lot of criticism from Blacks and from whites and from everybody about who I am and my image," Kelly said during a 1989 talk at the Fashion Institute of Technology. "And with the Blacks I always say, if we can't deal with where we've been, it's going to be hard to go somewhere."[59] Kelly made a decision to directly address racist iconography and engage with his Blackness through designs and in the persona he presented. "I design differently because I am Patrick Kelly, and Patrick Kelly is black, is from Mississippi."[60]

Born in Vicksburg, Mississippi, in 1954, Kelly spent a lot of his youth being brought up by his grandmother, Ethel B. Rainey, after his father died when he was fifteen. Rainey was a seamstress and maid, but his aunt was the one who taught him how to sew—the leap he took into fashion wasn't far behind. At first, Kelly moved to Atlanta in 1974 where he created window displays at the YSL Rive Gauche store and repurposed vintage clothes on the side. In 1979 he moved to New York City and enrolled at Parson's School of Design, becoming immersed after hours in the New York club scene. Eventually the pioneering fashion model Pat Cleveland, a friend and confidant, suggested he move to Paris.

It was against the romantic backdrop of the 80s that Kelly made his name. Celebrity clients like Grace Jones, Madonna, and Paloma Picasso wore his designs. He signed a worldwide deal with the Warnaco Group, leading to $7 million in sales. In 1988 he had the honor of being admitted to Chambre Syndicale du Prêt-à-Porter des Couturiers et des Créateurs de Mode, the governing body for the French fashion industry, gaining Chanel, Dior, and Yves Saint Laurent as official peers. The marketing logo he used in this period was a golliwog. His design signature was a mishmash of mismatched buttons—inspired by his grandmothers sewing solution when they couldn't afford the matching option—bright colors, tight silhouettes, rogue nipples popping out of jackets. Joy wrapped up in a dress.

Much has been made of Kelly's southern charm and manners, a little less has been made of the Jim Crow laws he grew up under in Mississippi where the sticky hands of slavery had fingerprints all over enduring rules of segregation. His use of golliwogs, the love lists he left at the end of shows revealing inspiration in fried chicken, and his collection of over six thousand black dolls were his way of confronting that history.

Patrick Kelly poses with models wearing
his colorful designs and signature buttons
[date unknown].

Back then, Black media like *Jet* magazine and *Ebony* magazine carried
features on Kelly, suggesting that he wasn't exactly persona non grata.
Certainly in today's environment, Black people understand that impulse
to tackle these racist tropes head on. Kelly summed it up perfectly in
an interview with *Vogue* in 1989, when discussing the complaints of
racism he received from Blacks and whites alike: "If you don't know
where you've been in your history, then you don't know where to go."[61]
Though his death was untimely in 1990, up until that point no one could
accuse Kelly of being directionless.

What of the relationship with these fashion designers and the Black
community now? For many, these legends have popped up in the
way that you discover a long-lost family member, and the response
is one of awe and wonder. Blackness is a culture where our elders are

respected simply for being elders, so when these men reappeared with their barrier-busting achievements, any issues that may have irked Black people at the time are reduced to nothing. There is a sympathy underpinning the admiration for all the effort it must have taken to operate in a world as the "only one" or some sort of pioneer, and with it an understanding that how you engage with your Blackness is an individual choice and should leave room for nuance. For today's designers: Are you a Dapper Dan marinating in all things ghetto? That is perfectly legitimate. More of a Willi Smith and preoccupied with your beautifully cut cotton trousers and having fun with a Keith Haring type? All fine. Or are you Patrick Kelley, resolute in confronting the racism that surrounds you? Also to be applauded. By the same token, there needn't be the expectation for the Black community to love the work of the Black individuals operating today. The freedom is not in "not seeing color" but in seeing it and not having assumptions about what it means.

LEFT: A model wearing a dice outfit by Patrick Kelly at his Ready to Wear Spring/Summer 1989 fashion show during the Paris Fashion Week, 1988.

CONTEMPORARY BLACK DESIGNERS AND VALUE DYNAMICS

We all want our work to be valued. Whether it's a child waving a stick drawing in front of a parent or an assistant quietly waiting for a manager's feedback, there is a need for recognition when we create and produce. For fashion designers, value and acknowledgement directly translates into status and sales; and historically those two north stars have been the goal. Make clothes, sell clothes, make money, win industry awards, be publicly celebrated, party, rinse and repeat. Being successful at all stages of this cycle is no simple feat for a modern Black fashion designer who wishes to operate in the top ranks of the industry. It's an expensive business—the training, the making of clothes—and without financial support, an almost impossible one. Selling clothes—or selling anything!—has now become so wrapped up in influencer marketing that it feels impossible to separate success from social media visibility—and the social world is still, mostly, a white world. The accumulation of plaudits for Black designers from peers and the public is rapidly improving, but it is still the white industry leaders who often dictate what deserves attention and praise. For all of these reasons, and others that are more difficult to unpack, value and Black design have a complicated relationship.

Influencer marketing is a tool that many Black designers feel they need to utilize to be seen. While the world of influencers is dominated by white women, it also kneads the value cycle I described into something less predictable. Designers such as LaQuan Smith are being supported by a combination of high-profile Black women and, less predictably, by Instagram-friendly white celebrities. He successfully utilizes the cache of the likes of Hailey Baldwin and the Kardashians while celebrating Black women in his shows and his imagery, popularizing a unique aesthetic that centers the female form.

In a 2015 *Vanity Fair* interview, Smith explains that he's felt boxed in as a Black designer. "I've been typecast. I still continue to get typecast. My name is LaQuan Smith, so it's fancy and then very dull, but you know, I guess when they hear the name they think urban."[62] He is aware that the Kardashians has been beneficial for his brand—in the same interview he recounts that his website crashed when Kim wore his dress—but what their endorsement also did was help to legitimize Smith's designs beyond the unwarranted "urban" label. There is this sense that if a Black designer's work is coveted outside of Black culture it is somehow "better" than work that is not. Related to this is a system where designs and processes that have long been present in Black culture are not anointed with any public value until used and distributed by white creators. Thankfully, there are Black designers who are correcting this by constructing an alternative system where the goal is not simply to sell clothes but to engage with their homes and communities. For example, the Nigerian fashion and textile designer Kenneth Ize creates his garments with local artisans in Ilorin State in Western Nigeria. Similarly, Sindiso Khumalo works with local women in Cape Town, South Africa, to alleviate poverty.

Today's Black designers are setting their own parameters for what value is. Black fashion cannot be reduced to one thinly disguised racist descriptor like "urban" nor can it be contained in the arcane cycle of financial gain and plaudits. What Black fashion creators are engineering is a kaleidoscope of intention and design that does not require the approving gaze of whiteness to be validated—they are being seen on their own terms.

INFLUENCERS AND THE ROAD TO VALUE

We talk about influencers today as if they are an entirely new phenomenon, when in truth, women and men of note have been having an impact on the livelihoods of designers for as long as labels have existed. What has changed is public awareness of the matter. When the noun "influencer" superseded the verb "influence," what was initially the domain of marketing speak slithered into the lexicon of mass media platforms and social conversations appearing as either a life goal or a sign of everything that's wrong with our society. So is "influencer" a dirty word? Well, it's definitely not clean. Most people taking issue with influencers argue that individuals are purporting to be "normal" and engaged with

"A CONSORTIUM OF INFLUENTIAL WOMEN OF ALL COLORS AND CREEDS HAVE EN- DORSED HIS CLOTHES"

brands while selling what is often an unattainable dream. These lifestyle influencers are typically racially ambiguous and well-proportioned with faces that showcase the beauty of symmetry. It's not hard to see why this has notes of the problematic, but this line of thinking does not account for the breadth of influencers, the scope of their work, or the role they play in the shining and refraction of light on Black designers. When it comes to emerging fashion labels that are typically independent and financially stretched, the right influencers parading their wares is the main weapon in their marketing arsenal. Consider then the Black fashion designer, a figure who is less likely to have connections in the industry, is seen as an unattractive financial investment and may well be starting from even more precarious financial footing. Influencers—or their less derided "celebrity" counterparts—can be integral to a Black designer's success. Case in point: LaQuan Smith.

In an article published by *Vogue Business*, LaQuan Smith, recipient of the 2021 CFDA/Vogue Fashion Fund, speaks at length about the importance of "social media storytelling." "As an independent designer, I don't have the means or the resources to crank out all this content [that Net-a-Porter have]," Smith says, referring to the business of his mentor, Alison Loehnis. "So [we're] having these conversations about how to grow, how to expand." He goes on to say "Social media, technically, is my best friend. That's the best tool that has helped me with my business."[63] Beyoncé was one of the first celebrities to wear LaQuan Smith, which led to further endorsements from Rihanna, the Kardashian-Jenner Klan, Lady Gaga, and Jennifer Lopez. A consortium of influential women of all colors and creeds have endorsed his clothes as being sexy and desirable and Smith has benefited hugely both in terms of his personal profile and in the value attached to his clothes. "Meet the It-Designer That the Kardashian-Jenner's Can't Stop Wearing" ran a 2015 headline on *InStyle* magazine's website.[64] In 2022, Smith was once again making *Vogue* headlines that referenced the women attached to his brand: "Looking for the Cool Girls? They Were All at LaQuan Smith's After-Party"[65]

Seeing the visibility and elevation of Smith and his designs being super-charged by influential women is a pleasure to watch. His clothes are unapologetically sexy and tight, providing a cat-woman silhouette that purrs power. And Smith's origin story also has superhero qualities: in his senior year at high school he discovered that he had fibrosarcoma, a type of bone cancer, in his left toe. While in the process of graduating and having treatment, he applied to the Fashion Institute of Technology and Parsons School of Design but was rejected by both. Unperturbed, he went on to design out of his grandmother's basement, launching the stratospheric career we see now.

Powerful fashion academics said no to Smith's vision while a guard of fashion influencers said yes. In an early interview, Smith suggests that the rejection may have stemmed from the admissions team not feeling that there was a market for his clothes: "Design schools were curious about his 'potential market' (read: ethnicity), and Smith wonders if that was a factor in his rejection."[66] It is unclear if the academics who rejected Smith included people of color, but there are whiffs here of the "urban" brush and the related misconceptions practiced by people who think either that Black people don't buy things or that white people don't buy things made by Black people. The point is, that without an alternative route for exposure, spearheaded by women of color but super-charged by white influencers like the Kardashians and Hailey Bieber, we may never have been privy to Smith's signature spectacles of strong women strutting the catwalk. Whether his models carry the oversized handbag proclaiming "I'M MOVING OUT" from his autumn/winter 2020 collection, or Julia Fox, hot off the heels of a Kanye breakup, strutting down the runway in a floor-length gown, Smith reciprocates the fame female influencers have given him by incorporating their life-style into his designs. His muse is "a woman who appreciates glamour; someone who is not afraid to dress up in the middle of the day just to run her errands 'like a boss woman should.'"[67]

Though Smith's relationship with influencer marketing has been a productive one, it is worth questioning if he would have received the same level of attention if his work had remained solely in the Black domain, or within the "potential market" that the design schools were so curious about. The statistics say that Black influencers are less valued, the implication being that their capacity to boost a brand is seen as holding less worth. MSL U.S. in partnership with the Influencer League found that just 23% of Black influencers (versus 41% of white influencers) made it into the macro influencer tier of 50k+ followers,

LaQuan Smith with models wearing his
unapologetically "sexy" designs, 2015.

and that the pay gap between white and Black influencers stood at
35%.[68] This correlates with the words of Elizabeth Castaldo Lundén in
the *International Journal of Media and Culture* where she argues that
"Web 2.0 has turned into a primarily commercial outlet, perpetuating
discourses of privilege and systems of commodity fetishization."[69]

Social media is largely positioned as a leveling force allowing marginalized groups to speak authentically to their audience. Theoretically,
Black designers can bypass fashion's gatekeepers and reach potential
customers with effective messaging and visual content. In this utopian
version of socials, we are all finally operating in a meritocracy where
the designs and the brand will speak for themselves. There are solid
examples of this: @telfarglobal, the brainchild of Telfar Clemens, is
an Instagram feed full of the joys of Blackness and has been integral
to the brand's global success. Similarly, LaQuan's Smith's short and
tight-tight aesthetic has benefited hugely from the famous women
of Instagram. And yet this seemingly utopian paradise holds murky
challenges for Black fashion designers beginning with Blackfishing.

"Blackfishing" was coined by Wanna Thompson in 2018 in a viral Twitter
thread. "Can we start a thread and post all of the white girls cosplaying

as black women on Instagram? Let's air them out because this is ALARMING"[70] was her call to arms. "White public figures, influencers and the like do everything in their power to appear Black," Thompson went on to explain to CNN. "Whether that means to tan their skin excessively in an attempt to achieve ambiguity, and wear hairstyles and clothing trends that have been pioneered by Black women."[71] The Kardashians and Rita Ora are cited as repeat offenders, with a variety of Instagram models and influencers keeping them company. The issue here is that those who are busy Blackfishing are rewarded for their efforts with levels of clout and cash that are denied to the Black people they borrowed the look from. In the same CNN piece, Leslie Bow, a professor of Asian American studies, states that "there is a specific power dynamic in American society that implies aspects of racial culture must be validated by those with status for them to be considered positive or valuable."

For aspiring Black fashion designers, Blackfishers add to their barrier of entry. When high street, fast fashion, and even some luxury brands are looking for collaborators who speak to the Gen Z audience they are trying to tap into, the white girl masquerading as Black is a more attractive proposition than actual Black girls. It is not a coincidence that Rita Ora has had fashion collaborations with everyone from Madonna's Material Girl line to Escada, adidas Originals, and Giuseppe Zanotti. Similarly, when you look at the opportunities in design that have been afforded to the likes of Molly-Mae Hague, a contestant in the ever-popular Love Island series who was accused of Blackfishing in her use of brown foundation, and is now the creative director for PrettyLittleThing, it is easy to come to the conclusion that white influencers with a Black aesthetic are in demand.

This pattern of Black aesthetics only achieving value status once embraced by white creators can also be seen in the complicated appropriation (or more kindly, the borrowing) of what is loosely described as "African print" but actually named African or Dutch wax prints, or Ankara. The difficulty is surmised wonderfully by Damola Durosomo in *OkayAfrica*: "Dear Western fashion houses, please stop taking designs that Africans have been wearing for years, calling them your own, and charging people out the ass for them. Thank you."[72] This request was prompted by Stella McCartney's 2018 spring/summer collection where she partnered with Vlisco, a longtime and well-known maker of Ankara prints. But her label is by no means the only fashion house to use the textiles in their designs—Comme des Garçons partnered with Vlisco in the past and so did Viktor and Rolf. In these cases, the lack of Black models used on the catwalk was rightly called out, but it's Durosomo's plea that speaks to the particular problem of value

Sketch by LaQuan Smith of a jacket and jumpsuit
outfit inspired by the *Black Panther* film, 2018.

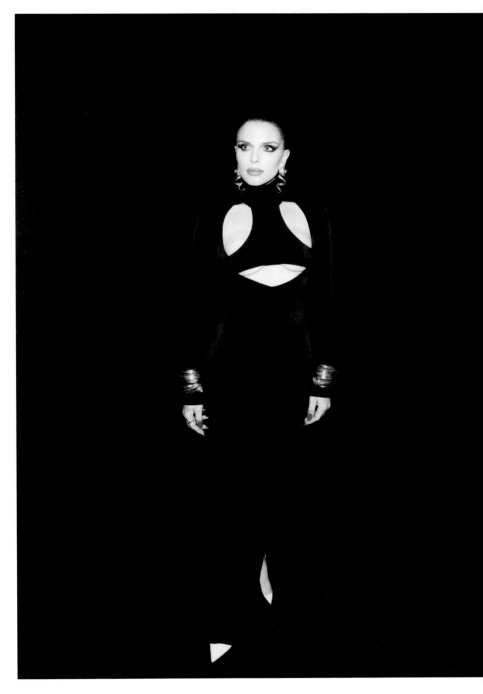

Actress and model Julia Fox wearing a black
dress designed by LaQuan Smith for his Fall/
Winter 2022 collection.

Model Naomi Campbell wearing clothes
designed by Kenneth Ize during Arise Fashion
Week in Lagos, Nigeria, April 2010.

upgrading of Black design in white hands. African designers have been
using Ankara prints for years, but their creations were not referenced
or reviewed by the fashion press establishment, and instead were
confined to African fashion weeks such as Lagos Fashion Week and
magazines such as *Arise* and *Nataal*, publications dedicated to the
African diaspora. Suddenly, when Ankara is taken out of context and
appears on the runway of a white designer, it becomes noteworthy in
broadsheets and established luxury platforms.

Depending on what camp you're in, it is either essential or irrele-
vant for me to mention what I thought to be quite an extraordinary
fact: the prints most associated with Africa are not made in Africa at
all—Vlisco wax prints are designed and manufactured in southern

Holland. Furthermore, the history of the print with Africa is knotty. In the nineteenth century, Dutch, British, and French companies were all attempting to dominate trade in the reproduction of Indonesian (then called the Dutch East Indies) wax printed batiks. The idea was to reduce the cost of creating the batiks by moving the dyeing process from handmade to automated. Though successful in this endeavour, the Dutch East Indies market did not demonstrate an appetite for the cloth. There are various stories of how the cloth then ended up in West Africa: Firstly, the romantic legend that West African soldiers who were employed by the Dutch army to expand colonies in Dutch East Indies took rolls of the cloth home in the late nineteenth century. The second, more provable narrative is that a demand for wax prints was communicated by Swiss missionaries to Scottish businessman Ebenezer Brown Fleming, who then shipped the first industrial batiks to the Gold Coast in 1893.

Vlisco, one of the more successful brands to emerge at this time, started creating the batik fabric in 1846 and are still the dominant player now. The colonial roots of their Wax Hollandais, Super-Wax, and Java brand have not gone unnoticed by scholars or designers. The Nigerian scholar Tunde Akinwumi argues in his 2008 paper "The 'African Print' Hoax" that "Using the term 'African Print' for [abada, Ankara, Real English Wax, Veritable Java Print, Guaranteed Dutch Java Hollandis, Uniwax, ukpo and chitenge] brand names is only acceptable to its producers and marketers, but to a critical mind, the term is a misnomer and therefore suspicious because its origin and most of its design characteristics are not African."[73] Similarly, a number of African designers refuse to use Dutch wax material in their work. As Malian-born indigo dyer Aboubakar Fofana says, he could "never agree with the use of wax print to symbolise African-ness."[74]

And yet the cloth does symbolize African-ness to the majority. "To some extent, the question of whether Vlisco is truly "African" or not is moot, because the fabric so readily and indelibly signifies the fashion and style of West African women; it might be like asking if denim is "really American" given the complex global history of indigo." wrote Sarah Archer in *Hyperallergic*.[75] Revered Nigerian artist Yinka Shonibare has woven it throughout his work, and it's become a mainstay in African-inspired homeware lines such as Bespoke Kinney. The argument is that these designs are now so inextricably entwined with African traditions and history that they *are* African.

In recent years, there has been a cluster of Black fashion designers who are reclaiming Ankara as their own. Brands like Boxing Kitten, a New York–based label cited for introducing Ankara to the American market, and Laviye, owned by British designer Abiye-Yvonne Dede, who was born in Nigeria, successfully produce Ankara print designs for a mass-market audience. While Sindiso Khumalo and Kenneth Ize, two of the most prominent African designers succeeding in the luxury space, are designing their own textiles from scratch.

South African Sindiso Khumalo is described as a sustainable fashion and textile designer. She rose to prominence in 2020 when she was one of eight finalists for the LVMH Prize for young fashion designers and received the Green Carpet Fashion Independent Designer Award. The clean lines and bold shapes of her designs nod to her dual training in architecture and textiles. Her prints, explicitly inspired by Africa and female empowerment, are as notable for their intricate handwoven and hand-embroidered detail as they are for the process with which they are created. Each garment is created with local NGOs in South Africa and Burkina Faso, where she seeks to raise women out of poverty by teaching them skills across embroidery, textile design, and pattern making. Underpinning this project is the belief that sustainability is rooted in economics and poverty elevation. "I feel the social and environmental sides of the sustainability conversation are inextricably linked, and as designers we need to try and address both where we can," Khumalo explained in an interview with *Elle* magazine.[76]

Kenneth Ize, the Lagos-based designer who made his Paris Fashion Week debut in 2020, shares a similar connection to local communities. That year, he purchased a plot of land in Ilorin State in Western Nigeria where he is constructing his own weaving factory near the artisanal *aso oke* weavers who create the textiles for his collections. As his collections have gone from bright and vibrant to earthy and tonal, what's remained is the exquisitely woven tailoring[77] admired by fashion critics. As with Khumalo, there has been a lot of hype around Ize—Naomi Campbell and Adwoa Aboah both walked his show, and he was a finalist for the LVMH Prize in 2019. Their designs stand alone as beautiful pieces of work but their philosophy—engage the community, evoke local traditions, revel unapologetically in Africa—points to a new era where Ankara is no longer the main indicator of African design. What Ize and Khumalo are doing is creating new systems through which luxury Black design is made and considered, and in doing so, they are reframing and broadening the indicators of African design. This is not an approach that can be packaged into a print and repurposed by white fashion designers. It is a new era. The Western fashion houses will not be able to call this their own while "charging people out the ass." Damola Durosomo's call has been answered.

Interestingly, neither Ize nor Khumalo are inextricably entwined with influencers. Instead, the Holy Grail of sales and industry recognition enjoyed by their peer LaQuan Smith is sought through a quietly radical approach that gives equal priority to uplifting and including local African

Sindiso Khumalo wearing her own
printed design, 2021.

communities and combining African-soaked artistry with stories of
Black culture woven into the designs. Without knowing the details
of their commercial revenue, we can assume that as relatively young
labels with limited supply, they are not making unspeakable amounts
of profit at this time. But the true test or their philosophy is whether or
not their principles lead to long-term, sustainable success that is both
financial and critical. Maybe part of the reason that the considered
routes they have taken mostly circumvent validation from white influencers is because they have utilized their imagination to redefine what
value means. This is not to say that the traditional success of LaQuan
Smith—fame, money, and acceptance—is not covetable, but it is not
the only form of achievement that exists in fashion. Maybe what we
can learn from Ize, Khumalo, and Smith is that Black designers should
have the agency to define their own parameters of value.

Sindiso Khumalo's Spring Summer 2022 collection 'Jagger' showcasing intricate hand-embroidery.

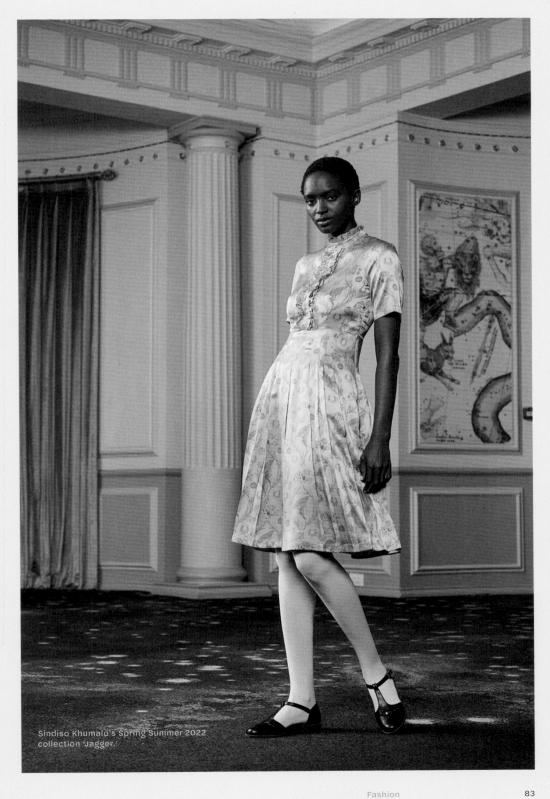

Sindiso Khumalo's Spring Summer 2022 collection 'Jagger.'

an education:
Bianca Saunders and Telfar

From time to time, those working in luxury fashion must defend the very existence of the industry and their roles to the general public. These instances can coincide with a big world event, but often out of nowhere, broadly taking three interchangeable, humorless forms: 1) people who care about clothes are vacuous and should be focusing on the more important things in life; 2) the industry is a rich playground and is completely disconnected from "normal" people; 3) high-fashion clothes are ridiculous and everyone looks ridiculous. There are too many comebacks to these arguments to list here—the contribution fashion makes to the economy, how clothes make us feel, fashion as an expression of self, to name a few—but one I will pursue is the role that fashion can play in educating people about cultures they'd otherwise be ignorant of. Clothes are an accessible portal to worlds that may otherwise go unseen. Decisions on materials, marketing campaigns, designer's references, and a designer's country of origin can all act as launchpads for stimulating interest in spaces, places, and things that have previously not been given due attention. With the absence of Black culture in histories taught, and a lack of depth in investigating Black culture now, clothes act as a gateway for raising awareness of specific moments of Blackness and Black experiences. Some designers are harnessing their positions and collections to shine a light on their worlds and there is nothing vacuous, disconnected, or ridiculous about their pursuits.

OPPOSITE: A model wearing Telfar's multifunctional, unisex designs, 2022.

TELFAR

Telfar's vegan leather tote, "the Bushwick Birkin,"[78] is "Not just for you — for everyone."[79] Embossed with a TC logo and globally beloved by cool kids and celebs, these bags start at $150, and once released sell out within hours. When Beyoncé was spotted with a white Telfar creation, there was enough Twitter chatter about the effect she would have on pricing that Telfar was compelled to release a statement: "Prices not Changing."[80] What may have started off as an attempt to ensure that regular people had access to Telfar products has become tinged with political weight. This political weight has been described by Shelby Ivey Christie, an ex-*Vogue* staffer and host of the Girl with the Bamboo Earring podcast, as "a mini-study on classism and race in fashion . . . The Telfar bags are at a super accessible price point which allows for a younger, more multicultural consumer base to attain them." She argues that "It's turning the idea that luxury is synonymous with exclusivity on its head. It's a lesson in how access can be granted or kept from certain groups in order to maintain the outdated idea of 'luxury' products."[81]

Campaign for a collaboration between Telfar and
Ugg on Telfar's signature shopping bags, 2023.

The sentiment is echoed by Telfar Clemens and the brand's creative director Babak Radboy: "Handbags, in particular, are this thing that is supposed to be an economic status indicator. Like–I'm 25 or 30 or 40 and I'm *doing OK*. We have a status bag that has nothing to do with that."[82]

By making the brand accessible and available for all, Telfar Clemens has created a wide and engaged audience for his storytelling platform that communicates a specific experience of Black, Liberian queerness that is also a universal message about acceptance and inclusion. When it was announced in 2021 that Telfar would design the Olympic team uniforms for Liberia and act as the official sponsor of the Liberian team, the brand also drew attention to an African country few knew about. With his unique take on one-shouldered tank tops, African lappa (traditional cloth used by men and women as wraparounds), loose tracksuits, and the "T" for Telfar emblazed across the front of the uniform, Clemens asked "What is Liberian fashion? It's not just putting kente print on a tank top. What does nationality even mean?"[83]—opening a Pandora's box into the history of Liberia and the experience of Liberian Americans.

The American Colonization Society, an organization founded in 1816 to facilitate the movement of free Black slaves back to Africa, transported approximately 2,800 former slaves to Liberia. When the country became independent in 1847, American fingerprints still remained: the country's motto, "The love of liberty brought us here"; the capital city of Monrovia is named after the fifth president of the United States (James Monroe); as well as the red, white, and blue stars and stripes that make up the Liberian flag. The nineteenth-century settlers were the dominant group for a century before Samuel Doe came to power in a military coup in 1980. In-fighting between different ethnic groups within the coup led to a bloody falling out in 1989, where the country, then led by President Charles Taylor, descended into a civil war where 1 in 14 Liberians died.

Shortly after being born in Queens, New York, in 1985, Clemens's family moved back to Liberia only to return to New York in 1990 as refugees. Initially the family lived with his aunt and various cousins in the LeFrak City housing complex in an area commonly referred to as Little Liberia before moving to Gaithersburg, Maryland, in 1993. Clemens messed around with making clothes as a teenager, but it's not until he moved back to New York in 2003 to study accounting at Pace University that he began to adapt vintage clothes and started making oversized T-shirts that were sold at Vice media's retail store. With that money, he started his label making multifunctional unisex attire that played with standard forms. "There's something *middle* about everything," said his friend and collaborator Ryan Trecartin. "Like a medium, like an average—but it doesn't make it less unique. It's like a mutant."[84]

This "mutant" includes creative collaborators from Ugg to Budweiser and is in a permanent state of disruption. What could have become chaos is instead a vibrant community of Blackness that poses questions about what it means to be American, gives space to the experience of being an immigrant, and puts the Black queer man front and center. The clothes are a delight but so is the presence of Telfar Clemens and the unapologetic world he's designed.

ANDROGYNY CENTERED

Bianca Saunders stepped into the scene creating a palpable frenzy of excitement that ricocheted across fashion with a reinterpretation of the Black male similar to Telfar. Contemporary fashion designer Saul Nash, said of her work: "The way in which she combines her culture in a timeless and authentic way. As a Londoner of Caribbean heritage, I had never really seen it approached with such a modern outlook before."[85] For Saunders's first collection, "Personal Politics," her androgenous silhouettes—initially modeled on the men in her family who she inter-

The Liberian Olympic Team wearing designs by Telfar for the opening ceremony of the Tokyo 2020 Olympic Games, 2021.

Bianca Saunders's Spring/Summer 2020
campaign, using her family as models.

"HAVING THIN BOUNDARIES BETWEEN WHAT IS SEEN AS MALE AND WHAT IS SEEN AS FEMALE CLOTHING IS REMINISCENT OF BLACK TRADITION"

viewed at length while designing the collection—contributed to an industry movement to upend norms of masculinity and instigated questions about how Black men are perceived and what societal restrictions had been placed on their identities. Lookbook images were of young Black men, poised and confident, in spectacularly detailed white T-shirts, puffer jackets, and sweatshirts with surprising ruffle adornments. They stand, mostly staring at the camera, in London destinations that are the antithesis of the postcard city we are used to seeing on film. This interpretation of London was textured and nuanced and evoked a sense of the Caribbean community that Saunders grew up in. Of equal importance was what these clothes and images said about being a Black man in a city that often made that status reductive. She has said that Black masculinity "should be a choice."[86]

The interrogation of Black masculinity continued with her subsequent collections. "Gestures" was created "to explore black male identity within the British culture and challenge the stereotypes of hyper masculinity,"[87] and "Unravelling" looked at Black men in their bedrooms and "conceptualised through the reflection of male figures in their most wholesome state and where they feel most open to self-expression."[88] Here was a designer telling us that the Black man can be feminine and that this does not bely their strength. In her mixed aesthetic where knitted jumpers come cropped without sleeves, tailoring is boxy with soft materials and unexpected color, and bomber jackets are paired with silk cloth, Saunders has painted a Black character in London that was largely absent in the public narrative and yet wholly recognizable within the Black community. It's an approach that won her the 300,000 euro ANDAM Prize in 2021 with mentorship by Balenciaga CEO & President Cédric Charbit.

Outfit from Bianca Saunders's Spring/Summer
2021 collection, "The Ideal Man," exploring the
complexities of male identity and masculinity.

Saunders's unpacking of what it means to be a Black male is contributing to a wider discourse taking place not just in fashion, but in TV, film, media, and art. Responses to literary work such as Paul Mendez's *Rainbow Milk*, a semi-autobiographical tale of a Black queer male, show that there's interest in the narrative of a Black man that is not rags to riches or evocative of other Black tropes. *Atlanta*, the genre-defining series created by Donald Glover, also speaks to the multitude of Black male characters and experiences with its quietly sensitive hip-hop star and his slightly preppy Ivy League cousin. A statement of intent by the previous editorial director of *Boy.Brother.Friend*, a magazine focused on Black male identity encompasses this new thinking: "We've set ourselves with the loftier task of destabilising inherited notions of masculinity, race, gender, the precariousness of sexuality, and the challenges posed by being with and being a male."[89]

Androgenous clothing designed by Saunders is an essential offering to this movement. Aside from being a sensible business move, having thin boundaries between what is seen as male and what is seen as female clothing is reminiscent of Black tradition, specifically African traditional wear where there is a long history of nonbinary attire. In Ghana, the Batakari (also known as a Fugu) is a smock worn by both men and women. Similarly, the Egyptian jalabiya is worn by both males and females. It's useful to point to the historic existence of gender neutrality in African garments because there is a pervasive view that toxic masculinity is part of Black culture when so many parts of Black society—the matriarchal family, the absence of gender specific language in some African dialects—suggests otherwise. Consciously or otherwise, the renaissance of androgyny is not the beginning of something new but the continuation of old traditions.

Culturally, Saunders's collections have also contributed to conversations on Black Caribbean culture. She describes a visit to the Somerset House exhibition *Return of the Rudeboy* as being a pivotal moment in her realising that Black Caribbean culture, *her* culture, was worthy of discovery and research as part of the design process. "I like that I can present a collection that is inherently about being Caribbean but doesn't have to be in yellow or green. I'm excited thinking about what men could put on their bodies—being sexy or even feminine, in a way."[90]

Following a BA in fashion at Kingston University, Saunders studied menswear design at the Royal College of Art where alumni like Philip Treacy (milliner), Christopher Bailey (Burberry), sculptor Henry Moore, and lifelong provocateur Tracey Emin loom large over the student body. Saunders has spoken of an environment supportive of anarchists and encouraging of expansive creative play with enthusiastic and original approaches to teaching, and yet the context for this experience is a space where Black students were unicorn-like. There is the impression that this otherness was balanced by the tight-knit community woven in South London around her immediate and extended family, the women of her mum's hair salon, and the omnipresence of Caribbean culture. The importance of family reflected in her younger brother and cousins have since featured in a campaign for her spring/summer 2020 collection "Nearness," photographed by Ronan McKenzie. The portraits evoke a sunny day at the beach with beach balls being replaced with melons and her younger cousins communicating the kind of adult assurance that comes from being surrounded by kinfolk. The picture most frequently picked up from the shoot shows the whole family, hair styled by Saunders's mother, framed around plastic black furniture, barely acknowledging each other's existence, which in itself evokes a strange sense of intimacy.

By evoking the deeply personal in her work—whether it's using the community of men she grew up with as a muse, the Caribbean culture that has informed her collections, or the inclusion of family in her campaigns—Saunders forces an assessment of her collection in the context of a community that she has defined. Collection titles like "Unravelled," "Personal Politics," "Henchmen," and "Character" are statements of intent as well as ideas to anchor her clothing in. As is the case with Telfar, the public musing over what Black male culture is versus how it has historically been presented requires those looking at Saunders's designs to take both her and her community in fully.

Law Roach
Charlene Prempeh

Law Roach is a former stylist. He is currently an image architect, the West Coast fashion editor for *British Vogue*, and a judge on HBO Max's voguing competition *Legendary*.

CP: How would you describe the current relationship between the fashion establishment and Black culture?

LR: That's a really interesting question, and I'm trying to answer just the best way I can. I think with the Black Lives Matter movement, the murder of George Floyd and how that affected the overall landscape of our country, as well as globally, I think we went into this phase of Black people, Black designers, and Black creators expecting and demanding more from the establishment. I think that some of the progress we've seen is because we have forced the hands of the powers that be.

I think we just started to stand up and say, listen, you've been profiting from us, stealing from us, mishandling us for this amount of time, and we're just not going to take it anymore. So you're going to respect our culture. You're going to give us the opportunities that we deserve. We're not asking you to give us anything other than what we earned. So I do think there has been change. But I also think that a lot of the change came because these brands and companies know that they can't thrive without our dollar and our input.

CP: What would you say has been the most positive change in the industry in the past few years?

LR: Just from my point of view, I think a lot of Black creative photographers, creative directors, stylers, hair, and makeup have been able to grow and expand and reach different levels of success in the industry, which I love seeing.

CP: When you think about the history of Black designers, what kind of patterns do you see being repeated? Good and bad?

LR: I think that Black designers were so few and far between throughout, let's say, the last sixty years. When I first came into the industry, the Black designer we had that we looked to was Tracy Reese. She was doing that New York Fashion Week, and it was just like her and no one else. It's that whole kind of problem of one at a time, like, it was one Black supermodel, one Black designer. Now I'm happy to see with the influence from Virgil Abloh and this new crop of young Black designers that's actually doing really well. And even if you look at it from the landscape of editorials, you see Black designers doing more editorials and more covers. Like, I literally just did the cover of *British Vogue* with Priyanka Chopra Jonas and LaQuan Smith. I think Edward Enninful has been doing a really amazing job of diversifying that magazine. For him to put LaQuan on the cover was a huge statement, because I felt like when it first started to happen, it was like, oh, let's mix some Black designers in just to check the diversity box. Now there are designers like Christopher John Rogers, LaQuan, Sergio Hudson, and Jerry Lorenzo at Fear of God. I think there's so many great Black designers right now that people can't deny the talent and the work. I think what kind of led that change is when I did the cover of *InStyle* magazine and used all Black everything—Black designer, Black hair, Black makeup. Every single look that Zendaya wore was from a Black designer. I think Laura Brown should be commended for being brave enough to let me do that. I think we are probably at a place where people respect the talent.

CP: You mentioned Black designers, but you've also talked about people, like editors, who are making changes. Often there's a real focus on the actual designers, but there's a whole network of people around them. Is there anyone other than the actual designers where you're like, that person is actually behind the scenes driving things and people just aren't aware enough?

LR: Yeah, because it's this thing in fashion, right, that until you meet somebody in person, you had no idea that they were Black. Especially in PR. It's because the landscape of PR is white woman dominated. So you can be emailing with someone for four or five years and you are finally at an event and they walk up and introduce themselves. You're like, oh, shit, you're Black! And I think even with me in my career, my industry is white woman dominated. It has been changing now, but I think we just had got accustomed to seeing one look, one face. PR is still a slow change, in my opinion. But then you also have people like Nate Hinton and Kevin McIntosh Jr.

CP: What does the future hold for Black fashion design? What do you see ten, fifteen years from now?

LR: I see a lot more. I see a lot more of us in that space. I'm waiting for the mega moguls to kind of pop up again, you know, like, reminiscent of what Pussy and Pussy did in the 90s, early 2000s, and Russell and Kamara. Like, I'm waiting for that, those billion-dollar brands. I feel positive and hopeful that that will come. So yeah, that's my dream and my wish.

ENDNOTES

01   Robin Givhan, "The Michelle Obama portrait is striking – and so is the gown she wore for it. This is its story," *The Washington Post*, February 12, 2018.

02   Debra D. Bass, "First Lady is Nation's Icon," *St. Louis Post-Dispatch* (MO), January 10, 2009.

03   Joy Miller, "Dapper Design for New First Lady Hopes to Glorify the American Look," *The Ogden Standard-Examiner*, January 6, 1960, p. 31.

04   President John F. Kennedy, "News Conference at Palais Chaillot, Paris," June 2, 1961, https://www.jfklibrary.org/archives/other-resources/john-f-kennedy-press-conferences/news-conference-12.

05   Amy Sullivan, *First Impressions: An Analysis of Media Coverage of First Ladies and Their Inaugural Gowns Jackie Kennedy to Michelle Obama* (The University of Alabama ProQuest Dissertations Publishing, 2018), p. 18.

06   Ibid.

07   Ibid, pp. 18–19.

08   Gerri Major, "Dean of American Designers," *Ebony Magazine*, December 1966, p. 137.

09   Judith Thurman, "Ann Lowe's Barrier-Breaking Mid-Century Couture," *The New Yorker*, March 22, 2021.

10   Letter from Ann Lowe to Jacqueline Kennedy, April 5, 1961. Clark Clifford Personal Papers, Box MF02 "Correspondence with Jacqueline Kennedy, 1961-1965," CCPP-MF02-002-p0025, https://www.jfklibrary.org/asset-viewer/archives/CCPP/MF02/CCPP-MF02-002?image_identifier=CCPP-MF02-002-p0025.

11   Ibid.

12   Ibid.

13   Allyssia Alleyne, "The untold story of Ann Lowe, the Black designer behind Jackie Kennedy's wedding dress," *CNN Style*, December 23, 2020.

14   Judith Thurman, "Ann Lowe's Barrier-Breaking Mid-Century Couture," *The New Yorker*.

15   Thomas B. Congdon Jr., "Ann Lowe: Society's Best-Kept Secret," *The Saturday Evening Post,* December 12, 1964.

16   Judith Thurman, "Ann Lowe's Barrier-Breaking Mid-Century Couture," *The New Yorker*.

17   Gary L. Lemons, "Black Fashion Designer Ann Lowe: Re(dis)covering the Life of the Nation's 'Best-Kept Secret'" in Sharon Kay Masters, Judy A. Hayden and Kim Vaz (eds.), *Florida Without Borders: Women at the Intersection of the Local and Global* (Cambridge Scholars Publishing, 2008), p. 72.

18   J.H. McGrew, "A Study of Negro Life in Tampa," typescript 1927. State Archives of Florida, Florida Memory, https://www.floridamemory.com/items/show/326639.

19   Ibid.

20   Ann Lowe on the *Mike Douglas Show*, 1964. Season 4, episode 44. Aired December 22, 1964, https://www.youtube.com/watch?v=wgZHWvmEqX8.

21   Gerri Major, "Dean of American Designers," *Ebony Magazine*, p. 140.

22   "Golden Fingers," *Daily News*, New York, January 21, 1965, p. 50, https://www.newspapers.com/clip/103073734/daily-news/.

23   Gerri Major, "Dean of American Designers," *Ebony Magazine*, p. 140.

24   Mary Clemmer Ames, "Life in Washington. Stories of the Late Slaves," *The Evening Post*, April 18, 1862, https://encyclopediavirginia.org/entries/life-in-washington-stories-of-the-late-slaves-april-18-1862.

25   Jennifer Fleischner, *Mrs. Lincoln and Mrs. Keckley: The Remarkable Story of the Friendship Between a First Lady and a Former Slave* (Broadway Books, 2004), p. 83.

26   Elizabeth Keckley, *Behind the Scenes: Or, Thirty Years a Slave, and Four Years in the White House* (G. W. Carlcton & Co., Publishers, 1868), p. xiii.

27   Ibid, p. xv.

28   Ibid, pp. 19–20.

29   David Robson, "Why some people are so talented," BBC, November 18, 2019.

30   Priya Elan, "Is 'streetwear' a dismissive term?", *The Guardian*, February 2, 2016, https://www.theguardian.com/fashion/2016/feb/02/is-streetwear-a-racist-term.

31   Siri Terjesen and Diamanto Politis, *From the Editors: In Praise of Multidisciplinary Scholarship and the Polymath* (Academy of Management Learning & Education, Vol. 14, No. 2, 2015), pp. 151–157, https://doi.org/10.5465/amle.2015.0089.

32 David Robson, "Why some people are so talented," BBC.

33 Angela Cotellessa, *In Pursuit of Polymaths: Understanding Renaissance Persons of the 21st Century*, (George Washington Universtiy, 2018), p. 216.

34 Ibid, p. 218.

35 Teresa Almeida, Erika Brodnock, and Grace Lordan, "Black women are missing from the UK's top 1%," *LSE Business Review*, March 3, 2021.

36 Zelda Wynn Valdes, "Oral History Project" conducted by Ed Schoelwer, May 4, 1995. Accessed via the New York Public Library, Dance Collection.

37 Nancy Deihl (ed.), *The Hidden History of American fashion: Rediscovering 20th-century Women Designers* (Bloomsbury Academic, 2018), p. 229.

38 M. Robinson, "New York Beat," *Jet Magazine*, September 10, 1953, p. 64.

39 Zelda Wynn Valdes "Oral History Project" conducted by Ed Schoelwer, May 4, 1995. Accessed via the New York Public Library, Dance Collection.

40 Laura Fox, "'It suits me way better': Rihanna hints her long-awaited next album will be 'completely different to how she wanted before' – after the singer cracked Forbes' Billionaires List," *Mail Online*, April 12, 2022, https://www.dailymail.co.uk/tvshowbiz/article-10711669/Rihanna-hints-long-awaited-album-completely-different-wanted-before.html.

41 Grace Wehniainen, "Savor Rihanna's Fenty Ketchup – Because New Music May Still Take A While," *Bustle*, August 24, 2022, https://www.bustle.com/entertainment/fenty-ketchup-will-hold-you-over-until-rihannas-new-album.

42 Sophia Kunthara, "Black Women Still Receive Just A Tiny Fraction of VC Funding Despite 5-Year High," *Crunchbase News*, July 16, 2021, https://news.crunchbase.com/diversity/something-ventured-black-women-founders/.

43 Jasmine Browley, "Two Black Women CEOs Make History on Fortune 500 List," *Essence*, June 7, 2021.

44 Donna Kelley, Mahdi Majbouri, and Angela Randolph, "Black Women Are More Likely to Start a Business than White Men," *Harvard Business Review*, May 11, 2021, https://hbr.org/2021/05/black-women-are-more-likely-to-start-a-business-than-white-men.

45 Oxford Learner's Dictionaries, https://www.oxfordlearnersdictionaries.com/definition/american_english/mainstream_1.

46 Rashaad Lambert, "'There is nothing minor about us': Why Forbes won't use the term minority to classify Black and Brown people," *Forbes*, October 8, 2020.

47 Matthew Schneier, "Gucci resurrects an 'undergroound' man," *The New York Times*, September 14, 2017. Section D, p. 1.

48 Jacob Gallagher, "Dapper Dan used to knock off Gucci, now he's collaborating with them," *Wall Street Journal*, May 14, 2012.

49 Vanessa Friedman, "The real lesson of Telfar, Kanye and the Gap," *The New York Times*, June 30, 2020.

50 David Marchese, "Dapper Dan on creating style, logomania and working with Gucci," *The New York Times*, July 1, 2019.

51 Lynn Darling, "Let them Wear Willi!", *Esquire*, December 1, 1984, p. 415.

52 Karin Eldor, "The New Age of Talent Developed: Elsa Majimbo's Secret Weapon, Mohamed Kheir," *Forbes*, August 25, 2021.

53 David C. Levy, email message to Julie Pastor, March 26, 2019 in Alexandra Cunningham Cameron, "Willi Smith Street Couture," Cooper Hewitt, https://exhibitions.cooperhewitt.org/willismith/about-willi-smith/.

54 Priya Elan, "Willi Smith remembered: the designer who introduced streetwear to the catwalk," *The Guardian*, June 8, 2020.

55 Jet, "WilliWear partner talks about future of WilliWear," *Jet Magazine*, May 25, 1987, p. 52.

56 Ki Hackney, "Willi," *Women's Wear Daily*, 124, no. 10, January 14, 1972, pp. 4–5.

57 Lynn Darling, "Let them Wear Willi!", *Esquire*, p. 412.

58 Ibid.

59 Patrick Kelly, "FIT Faces & Places in Fashion lecture series," Fashion Institute of Technology, New York, April 24, 1989, https://www.youtube.com/watch?v=-_gMSO_KjRc.

60 Nina Hyde, "From Pauper to the Prints of Paris," *The Washington Post*, November 9, 1986.

61 Julia Reed, "Talking Fashion: Patrick Kelly," *Vogue* (New York), 1989, 179(9), p. 778.

62 Elise Taylor, "Kendall Jenner Just Instagrammed Your Design. Now What?", *Vanity Fair*, September 16, 2015, https://www.vanityfair.com/style/2015/09/laquan-smith-kendall-jenner-kim-kardashian-designer.

63 Lucy Maguire, "Raising Star LaQuan Smith on Building an American Brand," *Vogue Business*, September 8, 2021, https://www.voguebusiness.com/fashion/rising-star-laquan-smith-on-building-an-american-brand.

64 Danielle Prescod, "Meet the It-Designers that the Kardashian-Jenners can't stop wearing," *InStyle*, August, 21, 2015, https://www.instyle.com/news/designer-laquan-smith-kim-kardashian-kylie-jenner.

65 Isiah Magsino, "Looking for the Cool Girls? They were all at LaQuan Smith's after-party," *Vogue*, February 15, 2022, https://www.vogue.com/slideshow/laquan-smith-nyfw-after-party-2022.

66 Studio Museum Harlem, "The Talented Mr Smith: Catching up with a Young Designer," Studio Museum Harlem [date unknown], https://studiomuseum.org/article/talented-mr-smith-catching-young-designer.

67 Taylor Stoddard, "Fashion Designer LaQuan Smith Finds Inspiration from Strong New York Women," *Forbes*, 2020.

68 MSL Staff, "MSL Study Reveals Racial Pay Gap in Influencer Marketing," MSL Group, https://mslgroup.com/whats-new-at-msl/msl-study-reveals-racial-pay-gap-influencer-marketing.

69 Elizabeth Castaldo Lundén, "Exploring Fashion as Communication: The Search for a new fashion history against the grain," *Popular Communication: The International Journal of Media and Culture*, vol. 18, issue 4, 2022, pp. 256.

70 Wanna Thomson @WannasWorld, "Can we start a thread and post all of the white girls cosplaying as Black Women on Instagram. Let's air them out because this is ALARMING," tweeted November 7, 2018, https://twitter.com/wannasworld/status/1059989652487069696?lang=en-GB.

71 Faith Karimi, "What 'Blackfishing' means and why people do it," CNN, July 8, 2021, https://www.cnn.com/2021/07/08/entertainment/blackfishing-explainer-trnd/index.html.

72 Damola Durosomo, "Folks are mad at Stella McCartney for ripping off designs that 'African Aunties' have been wearing for years," *Okay Africa*, https://www.okayafrica.com/africans-mad-stella-mccartney-ripping-off-african/.

73 Tunde M. Akinwumi, "The 'African Print' Hoax: Machine Produced Textiles Jeopardize African Print Authenticity," *The Journal of Pan African Studies*, vol. 2, no. 5, July 2008, pp. 179.

74 Clare Spencer, "Wax print: Africa's pride or colonial legacy?", BBC News, June 2022, https://www.bbc.co.uk/news/extra/4fq4hrgxvn/wax-print.

75 Sarah Archer, "How Dutch Wax Fabrics Became a Mainstay of African Fashion," *Hyperallergic*, November 3, 2016, https://hyperallergic.com/335472/how-dutch-wax-fabrics-became-a-mainstay-of-african-fashion/.

76 "Sindiso Khumalo on Sustainability and Winning GCFA's 'Independent Designer' of the Year," *Elle*, October 11, 2020, https://www.elle.com/uk/fashion/a34309243/fashion-designer-sindiso-khumalo/.

77 Maboro Seward, "Kenneth Ize finds light in the darkenss for AW21," *i-D*, April 11, 2021, https://i-d.vice.com/en/article/akdmm8/kenneth-ize-aw21-paris-collection-review.

78 Coined by makeup artist Xya Rachel in a September 2019 tweet. Quoted in Devine Blacksher, "How Telfar's Shopping Bag Became the Bushwick Birkin," *The Cut*, January 7, 2019.

79 Brand motto.

80 Telfar @telfarglobal, "PRICE NOT CHANGING. NOT FOR YOU – FOR EVERYONE." Temporary Instagram story, 2021.

81 Emma Hope, "Why the Telfar Shopping Bag is this decade's most important accessory," *Dazed Digital*, August 8, 2019, https://www.dazeddigital.com/fashion/article/45485/1/telfar-shopping-bag-it-bag-trend-identity-luxury-cfdas.

82 Ibid.

83 Vanessa Friedman, "How Liberia changed Olympic fashion—with a little help from a Brooklyn designer," *The New York Times*, July 24, 2021, https://www.nytimes.com/interactive/2021/07/23/style/telfar-liberia-olympic-team.html.

84   Emily Witt, "Telfar Clemens' Mass Appeal," *The New Yorker*, March 9, 2020, https://www.newyorker.com/magazine/2020/03/16/telfar-clemens-mass-appeal.

85   Finlay Renwick, "How Bianca Saunders became the beating heart of British Menswear," *GQ Magazine*, February 28, 2022, https://www.gq-magazine.co.uk/fashion/article/bianca-saunders-interview-2022.

86   Charley Brinkhurst-Cuff, "The Designer Challenging Archetypes of Black Masculinity," *AnOther Man Magazine*, August 18, 2017, https://www.anothermanmag.com/style-grooming/9980/the-designer-challenging-archetypes-of-black-masculinity.

87   Bianca Saunders, "Spring Summer 2019. Gestures," https://www.biancasaunders.com/spring-summer-2019.

88   Bianca Saunders, "Autumn Winter 2019. Unravelling," https://www.biancasaunders.com/autumn-winter-2019.

89   TJ Sidhu, "Boy. Brother. Friend: Examining male identities and the diaspora through art," *The Face*, May 28, 2020, https://theface.com/culture/boy-brother-friend-magazine-kk-obi-emmanuel-balogun.

90   Lynette Nylander, "Bianca Saunders is building a brand that does it all," *Frieze Week Magazine*, October 4, 2021, https://www.frieze.com/article/bianca-saunders-building-a-brand.

ARCH ITEC TURE

Introduction

When we've spoken about fashion and its relationship with Blackness in the previous chapters, it's been with the understanding that what we wear says as much about us as it says about the society we live in. The same is true for architecture: where we live can and should be another vessel for us to communicate what we value, and is inextricably entwined with the economic, political, racial, and environmental landscapes of our society. More personally, we know intuitively that moods and health are affected by the layout and design of our environments, a perspective rooted in theories such as salutogenic design that explore the capacity for space to reduce anxiety and promote positive psychological emotions. On the flip side, we also understand what happens when we exist within bad architecture. The feelings of claustrophobia that might arise from small, sterile buildings or how dull environments can make us feel depressed.

Considering the huge impact that space has on one's well-being, it's disturbing to think that Black people are far less likely to have control of their lived environment. In the UK, approximately 44% of Black households rent public housing[91] while in the US it's 48%.[92] This control is further lessened by the fact that in the US, only 1.9% of licensed architects are Black,[93] while the figure drops to 1% in the UK.[94] So not only is there difficulty in making intentional decisions about where to live, but the spaces that are created for us are not *by* us.

While the disparity in the above numbers is deeply troubling, in the chapters that follow I will focus on the work of the few Black architects who have been able to successfully reshape the relationship between Black people and the built space. By looking at America and the achievements of some of the first Black architects to emerge from the wreckage of slavery and segregation, as well as our forefathers and a new generation of African architects navigating a post-independence environment, a picture begins to form of an architectural landscape where hostility to Black professionals and Black design have conspired to reduce the progress of the Black community even as formal racist structures collapsed. Whether it's Paul Revere Williams placating white clients, or the various bodies and associations formed by African architects to ensure Black voices were given space, there has always been a parallel pursuit taking place for Black architects, where one lane involves the actual design of buildings and the other is cluttered with hurdles.

What's extraordinary is that despite the pressures that existed for these architects, from the macroeconomic issues of rebuilding Africa to the individual slights that were surely suffered, they produced not just imaginative and beautiful structures but a legacy of care for the Black communities they have sprung from. Paul Revere Williams designed the historic 28th Street YMCA building in 1926, which features bas-relief busts of African American heroes. Hilyard Robinson led the design of the Langston Terrace Dwellings in Washington, D.C. Norma Sklarek, known as the "Rosa Parks of architecture," was committed to mentoring young architects. John Owusu Addo was a founding member of the Ghana Institute of Architects (GIA). Oluwole Olumuyiwa advocated for Nigerian architects to be included in all public building projects. Demas Nwoko was part of a collective that developed a whole school of thinking on how to incorporate traditional African culture into art and design. Joe Osae-Addo is the chairman of ArchiAfrika, a platform that initiates and facilitates research on African architecture. Diébédo Francis Kéré has built schools in his local community with the participation of local people.

This list is not exhaustive—there are many other Black architects in America, Africa, and beyond who have achieved great professional success while progressing the position of Black communities and culture, but hopefully this survey is useful in provoking further discovery of an industry that can be opaque for the Black people that reside outside its parameters and problematic for those who exist within them. And yet the overarching takeaway for me was one of hope: the Black architects who have come before and the designers who exist now, have shown commitment to dismantling a hierarchy where Black architecture and professionals languish at the bottom of the pile. The ingenuity of Black culture is seeping into global structures and design theory through the momentum of Black architects. The future, at least for now, feels beautifully brown.

Paul Revere Williams and Respectability Politics

MTV Cribs was a masterpiece of television. I was mesmerized in 2000 as I stuffed warm popcorn into my mouth and watched as Snoop walked us through room after room of garish carpets and questionable sofa arrangements. Destiny's Child showcased a house that looked so unlived in that I was dubious as to whether any of them had seen it before. But my favorite, the apartment that beset a lifetime of unreachable goals, was Mariah Carey's Tribeca apartment in New York City with an in-house salon and a closet the size of most West Village dwellings. At no point during this did I wonder who the architects were of these shiny abodes, but the same voyeuristic instinct to nose around the haunts of the rich and famous is what first brought me to the celebrity homes of Black architect Paul Revere Williams. And there were many examples of his work from the 1920s onward, including many residences for Hollywood's elite. Frank Sinatra, Cary Grant, Lucille Ball, and more. In addition to his work on residential estates, Williams designed glamorous commercial projects such as the headquarters for MCA, the Saks Fifth Avenue department store on Wilshire Boulevard in Beverly Hills, and the luxurious Sunset Plaza Apartments.

With such an impeachable roster of clients, you would assume that Williams had found himself in that very special, mostly inoffensive category of a Black person whose extreme talent made their race invisible to white people. Will Smith possessed this before his hand landed on Chris Rock's face. Star athletes have it when they're on a winning streak and Whitney Houston had it before she collided with Bobby Brown. The problem with this illusion is that it only works if white people are not reminded of the truth that the talented individual has skin that is in fact brown. Paul Revere Williams helped to sustain this alternative reality for his white clients by learning to draw backward so he wouldn't offend by sitting next to them. He also walked around sites with his hands behind his back so there'd be no awkward moments where clients would have to negotiate shaking his hand. But Williams was a Black man, and in a 1937 essay for *American Magazine* titled "I Am a Negro," he made it clear that the politics of being a Black male architect was not something he shouldered lightly.

Williams was born in 1894 into a middle-class family in Memphis, Tennessee, and first came to Los Angeles when his father attempted to start a fruit business. By the age of four, Williams and his brother lost both parents to tuberculosis, leaving the two in the care of the state. This is not a beginning that one might typically associate with a man who would become the first Black person to be (posthumously) awarded the American Institute of Architect's highest honor, the Gold Medal, but the brothers were adopted by loving but strict Black foster parents who were devoted to their education.

At age six, Williams took his first steps in learning to contend with being the only Black person in the room as the sole African American student at his middle school. He went on to graduate from Polytechnic High School in Los Angeles. The solid academic foundation and membership in the Los Angeles architectural club allowed him to pursue a self-directed education in architecture while participating in training and competitions offered through the Los Angeles branch of New York's Beaux-Arts Institute of Design. During this time, he worked with the firm of landscape architect and planner Wilbur D. Cook. However, it took an additional four years before he studied architectural engineering at the University of Southern California. What's immediately striking about this period is how self-motivated Williams was. In between the competitions and education, there was time employed at Pasadena Architect, a studio noted for luxury homes and "true California style" spaces. Williams even managed to certify as a building contractor in 1915 and is listed in the March 30 issue of *Los Angeles Builder and Contractor* as the designer for a two-story commercial building completed for Louis M. Blodgett, an African American millionaire, for whom Williams would later build two new homes.

The postgraduate trajectory is no less impressive. In 1921, he became the first officially certified Black architect in California before adding the Districts of Columbia, New York, and Tennessee to the list of states where he was registered. When the *LA Times* described him as "one of

Lucille Ball and Desi Arnaz House, Palm Springs,
built 1954–55, Paul R. Williams (architect);
photography 1955.

Southern California's best-known architects,"[95] it was fully warranted. During the Wall Street Crash of 1929, when most people were struggling to stay out of poverty, he continued to design homes for the wealthy, building one of his most impressive structures, a 12,000 square-foot home for horse breeder Jack P. Atkin. The brief was to design a castle on a hill that would bring back "memories of his childhood in England."[96] That childhood came alive as a 16-room Tudor Revival–style residence in Pasadena built in brick with a slate roof. Applying a suite of expensive materials—oak, marble, custom-designed stained and leaded glass, and In-Vis-O roller screens for windows—at Atkin's request, the house was eventually rented to movie studios, providing the locations for films like *Topper* (1937) and *The Bells of Stq* (1945). By 1934, Williams had completed over thirty-six residential estates.

This makes the timing of his essay "I Am a Negro" more provocative as it was done as a time of great success. In the essay, Williams details the lengths he went to in order to achieve success and the various setbacks and sacrifices involved in his journey. When white clients would come in and swiftly try and exit on discovering that he was Black, he would pretend that his prices were outside their budget in order to continue the dialogue. After one introductory meeting, he stayed up for twenty-three hours in order to submit a proposal before his white competitors could gain an edge. Williams punctuates these stories with a steady crescendo of wins and a persistent request that he should be treated as an individual and measured on his merit.

> "My hope for success was based largely upon my conviction that racial prejudice is usually blind, that it is less often the result of reason and personal experience than the offspring of inherited ideas and a hasty, American tendency to lump all things which look alike into a single category . . . And while I felt the futility of any attempt to break down their aversion to my race, I believed that if I could shock, or startle, or in any way induce those white people to regard me, not as 'just a negro,' but as Paul Williams, an individual Negro, I might then be able to sell my ability."[97]

He is also quick to point out his individual achievements and that of other Black people battling the status quo.

> "When I look about me and see the magnificent strides which so many men and women of my race are making, when I see the sacrifices they are undergoing in order to help other members of our race who deserve and need help, and when, remembering the burden of my own handicap, I realize the burden of theirs."[98]

All of this striving and achievement is unambiguously impressive, but it's also indicative of a facet of Black culture where it is assumed that

"My hope for success was based largely upon my conviction that racial prejudice is usually blind"

success requires a relentless work ethic rarely demanded from white peers. As Black children, many of us were brought up with the mantra that we have to work "twice as hard for half as much," as if it was a fact as clear as day rather than a situation thrust upon us by a lifetime of inequity. The idea overlaps with terms like "Black excellence," which, though positive in intention, create either the sense that Black people being excellent is exceptional in some way or that being educated and driven is a prerequisite to being valued as a Black person. The issue of respectability politics is also relevant here. In Professor Evelyn Brooks Higginbotham's 1993 book *Righteous Discontent: The Women's Movement in the Black Baptist Church, 1880–1920*, she spoke about "politics of respectability" as she examined the use of respectability narratives by Black baptist women to "counter the images of black Americans as lazy, shiftless, stupid, and immoral in popular culture."[99] Though she was focused on women the meaning is still valid to all Black people who find themselves in a position of needing to demonstrate "value" when that value is wholly defined by the morals and structures of white society. In Paul Williams's quest to become a successful architect, he dealt with incredulity that a talented architect could be Black. All the while, he carried himself with dignity and presented himself and his work as a living counterargument to tropes of Black people being incompetent.

There is a certain amount of awe reserved for all architects and doctors based on the implicit understanding that it takes a certain level of intelligence and academic diligence to enter these professions. While this halo effect bestows some residual respect on the Black architect, there is also a tendency to paint these individuals as a one off, as alien in some way. A similar philosophy is present when Black people show talent in sports or entertainment—it's the sense that their talent strips them of their Blackness and that being colorless is a worthy goal. Consider again the reaction to Will Smith slapping Chris Rock at the Oscars. There was a wealth of responses but some of the most troubling were that his actions would set back all Black people across the world. There is literally no white man anywhere wondering if Harvey Weinstein's sexual transgressions are going to affect how they are seen by the public or if it might cause a setback for all white men in the film industry.

Paul Revere Williams was indisputably exceptional and extraordinarily talented when measured against all his peers regardless of race. His achievements were also due to his hard work. Where race must be considered is when it comes to what form that hard work takes and how it differed for Williams and continues to differ for Black people when trying to operate in prestigious professions. Not only must we ask where the energy Williams spent placating his white clients could have been redirected, we should also question what versions of his sketching backwards takes place in professional environments for Black people in architecture today and what measures can be put in place to correct the need to employ contortionism in order to succeed. In "I Am a Negro" Williams demands, "Negroes—WAKE UP! The emancipation which was given you was only an opportunity. Real emancipation lies in your own intellectual effort!" He then cries, "White people—WAKE UP! A race is beginning to stir beneath your feet and to demand a place in the sun—*its* place, mind you, not yours."[100] The relevance of this quote nine decades later is not something to be celebrated. As a race, we are still stirring, still trying to find our place in the sun and for that spot to not be defined by whiteness and our capacity to adhere to terms of respectability and value we have had little hand in.

ABOVE: Paul R. Williams standing in front of The Theme Building, LAX, 1965. Williams was one of the architects at Pereira & Luckman to work on the project.

RIGHT: Beverly Hills Hotel, built 1949–50, Paul R. Williams (architect); photography 1950.

Norma Sklarek and Being the First

In 1959, Norma Sklarek became the first African American woman to become a member of the American Institute of Architects. Three years later, she became the first Black female licensed architect in California. By 1985, Sklarek was the first African American woman to co-own an architectural practice. This trio of firsts has caused some to anoint Sklarek as the "Rosa Parks of architecture," drawing parallels between Parks's commitment in protest and Sklarek's professional resilience. Today she is rightly celebrated as an architect who broke boundaries and penetrated a system that was not accepting of women and even less enamored with Blackness. There however needs to be some distinction between honoring Sklarek as a Black woman who achieved great things in a difficult context and the act of celebrating Black "firsts."

The significance of being the first dawned on me when I told my extended family that I was going to Oxford University to study politics, philosophy, and economics. Mostly the news was met with congratulations, but the unofficial patriarch and historian of the family, Dr. Fodow—who was the first member of the family to attend university—paused for an uncomfortably long time before suggesting that we have lunch. Broke and perennially smitten with free meals, I agreed to meet in a restaurant in Mayfair where my uncle painstakingly explained what it had taken for my grandmother and her sisters to get the funds together to send him to boarding school in Kumasi, Ghana, and how

Gold Medalist

Miss Norma Merrick, daughter of Dr. and Mrs. Walter Merrick, 1845 Seventh Avenue, New York City. Miss Merrick graduated last month from Junior High School, 93, and took the test for Hunter College, High School. She came out first in her class and won the most coveted honor—the Gold Medal. She made the highest marks in Algebra, 100 per cent. The Christian Courier congratulates this brilliant young student, and her parents. We wish for her continued success.

LEFT: News clipping in the *Christian Courier* about Norma Sklarek winning the coveted Gold Medal for coming first in her class in the entry exam for Hunter College High School [date unknown].

BOTTOM: News clipping of Norma Sklarek on her graduation and future plans, 1950.

Iris Collins   N. Fairweather   Betty Wilkins   Gladys Taylor

Norma Merrick Fairweather, 24 year old daughter of the Walter Merricks of Brooklyn, is the first woman of color to be graduated from the School of Architecture, Columbia University. Mrs. Fairweather displayed unusual ability in mathematics when a student at Joan of Arc High School and was advised by the late Vertner Tandy to study architecture. She also attended Hunter College High School and Barnard College. During her junior year in the School of Architecture, she spent some time in the Washington office of Hillyard Robinson where she received valuable, practical experience.

After a lavish graduation party last Friday evening at the home of her parents, Mrs. Fairweather and her husband, Lt. Benjamin Fairweather, an administrative assistant in the Medical Corps at Fort Dix, left on a holiday. When they return in the Fall, Mrs. Fairweather will be associated with a New York firm, and the only Negro woman actually working in the profession.

* * *

that sparked a chain of events that had led to this moment: I was the first member of our family to attend Oxbridge. Mostly I felt pride. The specific experiences and sacrifices of any one family that build into generational progress are moments to delight in, but I see that as quite different to the advancement of an entire race. In a world that wasn't beset with racism, Blackness would not serve as an indicator of your life outcomes. It would be no more outstanding that a Black person was James Bond than it would be that a Black person was a basketball player. Being the first Black individual to do something is not unequivocally a moment of collective celebration. If anything, it should cause us all to reflect on a system that is structured in a way where Black visibility in coveted arenas—such as that of architectural design—takes on unicorn status. When I look at the life of Sklarek and the number of rejections she received in her path to success, my attention is arrested on the failings of an industry that still struggles to welcome Black women into the fold.

Born in 1926 into a family of first-generation Caribbean immigrants, Sklarek grew up in Harlem at a time when the mass migration of Black Caribbeans to New York saw the group make up one-third of the Black population in New York City. It was also a moment when Black Caribbeans were participating in racial politics by creating periodicals. Marcus Garvey, who'd arrived from Jamaica in 1916, and his wife Amy Ashwood Garvey, had founded the Pan-African activist paper *Negro World* for the Universal Negro Improvement Association and African Communities League (UNIA-ACL), which at its peak reached a circulation of 200,000. Other notable Caribbean activists of the time were Eric Walrond, celebrated Harlem Renaissance author of *Tropic Death* and Claude McKay, Fabian socialist and poet.

The reality for Sklarek, living in poverty with numerous relatives in Harlem, before moving to Brooklyn, was not one of political agitation. Her parents were focused on ensuring that she received the very best education, resulting in two tactical moves: firstly, Sklarek converted to Catholicism in order to enroll in one of the better private schools in the area, which she attended until the sixth grade; secondly, when it was time for Sklarek to go to high school, her father befriended a woman on the Upper West Side and used her address to allow Sklarek to take the entrance exam to get into Hunter College High School (an institution for gifted students), the result of which was that Sklarek received the top score and was admitted into the school. Even at Hunter High, Sklarek experienced resentment and dismissal. "The . . . school that I went to was like 98 percent white," she recalls. "I was aware that the other students and the teachers considered me an inferior human being."[101]

Brushing off the discomfort of white people who could not stomach her brilliance (or chose not to see it) became Sklarek's superpower. Later, when she chose architecture as her professional pursuit, it took twenty interviews for her to eventually gain a role at the New York Department of Public Works where she was hired as a junior draftsperson. This despite the fact that she'd graduated from Columbia University with a BA in architecture with an impeccable academic record. Her ability to keep her eye on the prize—she has said that she was more interested in being an architect than she was in spending her life responding to either racist or sexist behavior in the workplace—allowed her to persist where feelings of insult may have overwhelmed others. The combination of this resilience and her work ethic catalyzed the many "firsts" that she achieved, and she was keen to pass these learnings on. "In architecture, I had absolutely no role model. I'm happy today to be a role model for others that follow," Sklarek said of her extensive mentoring and lecturing in the 1990s at Howard and Columbia universities and elsewhere.[102]

11   TERMINAL ONE, L A X

11 Terminal One, LAX designed by Norma Sklarek
[date unknown].

The modernist design of the US Embassy in Tokyo in 1976 and the Terminal One station at the Los Angeles International Airport in 1984 are often referenced as Sklarek's architectural successes. Of the latter she remembers the reticence of other architects to have her as the project director. "At first, the architects working on the airport were skeptical because a female was in charge of the project," recalled Sklarek. "But a number of projects were going on there at the time and mine was the only one on schedule."[103] Yet the act of one individual being able to negotiate a dysfunctional system says something brilliant about the person and something dangerous about the grounds that they operate in. Sklarek as an individual was not able and should not be held accountable for changing the game, she instead circumvented the hurdles. Now, years later, the barriers have not collapsed. Only 0.4% of registered architects in the US are Black women.[104] This is the danger of the "first" narrative—while we're blinded by the brilliance of one individual the failings of the system can persist.

MULTIPURPOSE BUILDING
COMMONWEALTH AVENUE ELEMENTARY SCHOOL

SIEGEL SKLAREK DIAMOND
A.I.A. ARCHITECTS

Drawing, Multipurpose Building Commonwealth Avenue Elementary School Siegel Sklarek Diamond [date unknown].

Hilyard Robinson:
A Room of Our Own

An extract from *The Negro History Bulletin* of April 1940:

> "In addition to technical proficiency the architect with thorough
> modern training is reinforced with fundamental understanding
> of broad social and economic factors that influence his work. This
> latter thought is important. It has been heretofore commonly
> thought that the architect's practice being limited therefore to
> the top of purchasing power. There is a larger function for the
> architect, and especially for the Negro architect. The general
> need for his services has grown immensely in recent years . . .
> [T]he Negro architect may become a determining force and
> indispensable factor in the struggle for more abundant living."[105]
> —Hilyard Robinson, Architect

Trained architects are no longer the gatekeepers to building design;
artists, designers, spatial practitioners, and technologists have all risen
to prominence as contributors to—and critics of—physical space. As
the scope of voices contributing to the discourse of architecture has
grown, the chorus has become marginally less defined by the white male
perspective as Black voices—trained architects and otherwise—attempt
to connect the spaces that we dwell in as they push for participation
in determining what these spaces are. Organizations such as MAIA, an
artist-led social justice initiative in Birmingham, UK work with artists to
develop spaces. RESOLVE, based in London, acts as an interdisciplinary
design collective that combines architecture, engineering, technology,

OPPOSITE: Langston Terrace Housing Project,
Washington, D.C., 1986.

and art to address social challenges. But as the territory of architecture and space is claimed back by initiatives seeking to support the Black community, it remains worthwhile to survey the forefathers of this movement. It is men such as Hilyard Robinson, who helped to utilize buildings as a tool for social good among Black people, and there are many facets of his work that remain inspirational and relevant to the cause today.

Robinson's activity in public housing reflects the political urgency in his writing. It also communicates the faith he had in the capacity of his Black community to appreciate the quality of buildings and to participate in the joy that they can give. The Langston Terrace Dwellings, a public housing project designed by Robinson, was a living, breathing example of that belief. His entire career spoke to a conviction that buildings might be the catalyst to a more equal and safer space for Black people. There has been some recent recognition for the innovative modernist designs created by Robinson. What should stand alongside this appreciation of his craft is a deeper understanding of his philosophy.

The experience of thriving in Black institutions would have played some role in developing Robinson's resolve to elevate the circumstances of his fellow Black people. He started his life in Washington, D.C., in 1899 as part of a working-class family. In 1917 he graduated from the prestigious M Street High School, one of America's first high schools for Black students. A lack of adequate funding meant that facilities and space were restricted, but the school had an excellent curriculum and a faculty peppered with individuals who contributed significantly to furthering the position of Black Americans, including former principals Francis L. Cardozo, the first African American to hold a statewide office in the United States, and Anna J. Cooper, a revered academic frequently referred to as the "mother of Black feminism."

It makes sense that after completing his bachelor of architecture at Columbia University which he started in 1924, he began to teach part time at Howard University, a relationship that would continue through the 60s and evolved into Robinson designing several of their campus buildings, including the School of Architecture-Engineering. M Street as a Black high school and Howard as a historically Black University or College (HBCU) shared an approach that prioritized academic excellence as well as responsibility to the community. The continued existence and success of Howard University can be attributed to some of the values Robinson expressed in his address to readers of the *Howard University Record* in 1925:

> "Do not be deceived into believing that Architecture is a luxury and an indulgence for the moneyed people alone. Nothing could

Hilyard Robinson working on plans and
specifications for one of two war-housing
projects at Ypsilanti, Michigan, 1939-1945.

be more erroneous. Good Architecture is not measured in terms of dollars and cents; its merits lie in the brain and experience of the architect, who—and I implore your confidence in this statement—is a most inexpensive servant, and besides, who—if he is of the proper temperament and efficiency—loves his work."[106]

The suggestion is that prestigious disciplines and environments are open to Black people, that engaging in these disciplines should in part be an act of service, and that as Black people we deserve to love what we do passionately. Fostering a sense of dignity and appreciation for Black culture in this way is as essential to the agenda of HBCUs as academic excellence and fully embraced as the bedrock of Robinson's agenda. There are people who object to institutions such as Howard on the basis that segregation should not be an answer to inequality and is in fact a hindrance to that very goal, but the roll call of successful alumni—Vice President Kamala Harris, Martin Luther King, Jr., Oprah Winfrey, and Spike Lee, among many others—undermines that line of critique, and arguably what they are really objecting to is the self determination that these spaces encourage. The practice of Hilyard Robinson, specifically his work on Langston Terrace Dwellings, a pioneering public housing project that revolutionized the living experience of its Black residents, adopted the notion that architecture designed by Black people for Black people might be the stimulus for a more gratifying Black future.

It was in 1931 when Robinson embarked on an eighteen-month subsidized tour of Europe after taking a leave of absence from Howard University and completing his master's degree at Columbia University. At the time, Sweden was busy building Barnrikehus, midrise modernist buildings for low-income families. In Rotterdam, the Kiefhoek housing estate had recently been completed by modernist architect J.J.P. Oud around 1930, a public housing project comprised of long rows of standardized two-storey units. The UK had already built the Boundary Estate in 1900, arguably the world's oldest public housing plan. Shaped by these public housing trends, Robinson was well placed to support the newly established Public Works Administration in 1935, created primarily to build public housing for the poor. In his role as chief architect alongside two local white Washington architects, Irwin Porter and Alexander Trowbridge, as well as the prominent and well-connected Black architects Paul R. Williams and his former boss Vertner Tandy, Robinson led the response to a brief asking for the design of the first federally sponsored public housing development in the nation. The proposal would birth the Langston Terrace Dwellings in Washington, D.C.

With the stigmas and issues that have come to plague public housing since, it can be a struggle to remember that the original intention was to provide a dignified space for people of lower incomes, and in the case of Langston Terrace, specifically Black people of lower incomes.

As noted by *Harvard Design Magazine*, "Langston Terrace arose out of the movement to provide not only safe and sanitary housing for working-class and poor people, but also housing that would uplift the spirits of its residents."[107] Its name paid homage to ideals of Black freedom and empowerment by honoring John Mercer Langston, abolitionist and founding head of the Howard University Law School. Robinson applied a modernist perspective shared with European and Euro-American architects that used open space and communal intersectionality to elevate the experience of residents. The sleek, aesthetically pleasing low-rise buildings encompassed 274 residences. Robinson also worked closely with prominent landscape specialist David Augustus Williston (the first professionally-trained African American landscape architect) to erect a central courtyard common featuring a large terra cotta frieze titled *The Progress of the Negro Race*—depicting African American history from slavery to World War I migration—and playgrounds dotted with large animal sculptures. Noted children's book author Eloise Greenfield became a resident at nine years old and remembers the sculptures as "friends to climb on or to lean against, or to gather around in the evening. You could sit on the frog's head and look out over the city at the tall trees and rooftops."[108]

For Robinson, his race may have better qualified him for the Black occupants on low incomes, but his legacy speaks to a more universal appreciation and advocacy for the dignity of the Black community. The response from those who lived there is not simply an appreciation for beautiful architecture, but also relief at having the opportunity to realize who they were. This petition for a Langston Terrace home embodies that hope:

> "We are very anxious to get settled in a nice home in a decent neighborhood where we can bring up our child successfully and make desirable friends. Langston Terrace seems to be our only hope because it aims to offer these advantages for a comparatively low price, one that we can afford to pay."[109]
>
> —Mrs. Joseph H. Middleton to the director of housing, December 1937

This speaks to the hope that Langston Terrace encouraged and the limited options of the time. Robinson asked if we could afford to "let progress trample over us," and he definitively answered in the negative with a building that acted as a catalyst to propel Black people to improved standards of living. For a time, those who experienced his buildings were elevated. Robinson's work serves as inspiration to generations of Black people to believe that they deserve beauty and the nourishment that the elegance of buildings can provide.

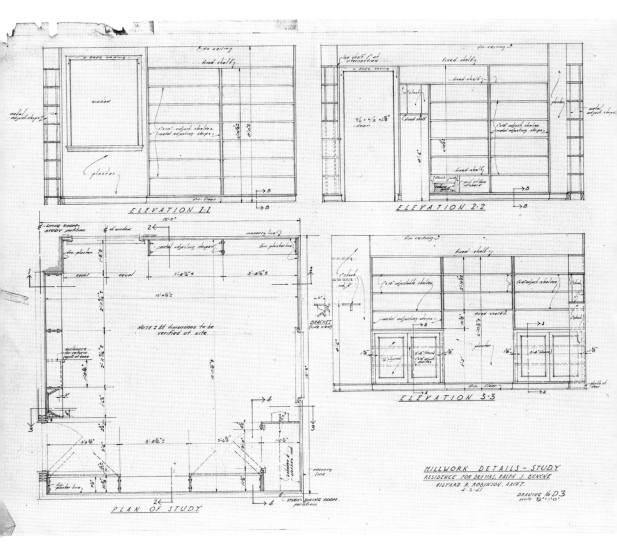

OPPOSITE: Ralph J. Bunche House, Washington, DC, designed by Hilyard Robinson.

ABOVE: Architectural drawing by Hilyard Robinson for Ralph J. Bunche House, 1510 Jackson Street Northeast, Washington, DC, July 1940.

Welcome to Africa

"Today, from now on, there is a new African in the world! That new African is ready to fight his own battles and show that after all, the black man is capable of managing his own affairs."[110]
—Kwame Nkrumah, March 6, 1957, Ghana Independence Day

Every Ghanaian has been told over a plate of jollof, some chicken, and a spicy beef kebab that Ghana was the first African country to gain independence. This is not strictly true. Liberia gained independence from America in 1847. Ghana was the first sub-Saharan country to gain independence. It was also the first county to break away from the insidious clutches of European colonialism.

As a card-carrying Ashanti from Kumasi (we are a bit like New Yorkers of Ghana—confused that Kumasi is not the capital city and enamored with our own legend), Ghana's status as a pioneering breakaway African state has always been a point of pride for me, and the story is passed down like a folktale to all of us in the diaspora. Yet there can often be an absence of detail in these oral histories, as well as a failure to elaborate on what was happening with our powerful neighbor two doors down in Nigeria. There is not the space to fully correct that here, but an exploration of architecture and the role it played in postcolonial restructuring is a reasonable starting point in understanding the dynamics of that era and the role of infrastructure in rebuilding and redefining West Africa. The stark narrative is one of identity and how African architects have tried to wrestle back the techniques and materials of their countries as a design language to communicate the value of West African culture. The great battleground was the artificial separation of African communities from the spaces they lived in, the belief that great architecture could not be generated from African

OPPOSITE: A crowd in Ghana welcoming a political prisoner, who was released during the coup which led to the overthrow of Kwame Nkrumah, 1966.

culture, and the long held colonial practice that civilization, beauty, and sophistication were attributes that needed to be imported into Africa. The work and perspectives of John Owusu-Addo, Oluwole Olumuyiwa, Demas Nwoko, Joe Osae Addo, and Diébédo Francis Kéré repudiate these stale notions of African architecture. In different ways, they have all addressed and diminished the colonial grip on West African spatial design by recapturing the essence of local culture in their practice, both in how they have worked and what they have created. As African architects, they are not alone in their attempts to contradict false narratives of what Africa is—there is a sea change happening in design and in other disciplines across the continent that is positioning Africa as fiercely and proudly independent.

ARCHITECTURE DURING GHANA AND NIGERIA'S COLONIAL BREAK

There are moments in history when the consensus is that everything will change, and then things do not. For Black people, these false starts have been numerous. Slavery ended and shapeshifted into segregation. When the latter ended legally, it did not end culturally. Many argue that when the former ended in public, it simply moved venues and set up shop in prisons. Across the Atlantic in West Africa, there have been similar stutterings, most notably, the victory of independence.

It was March 6, 1957, when Ghana, named after the title given to the ruler of the precolonial West-African Wagadou empire, was formally separated from the colonial occupation of Great Britain. Founded by Kwame Nkrumah, a returning student from both the US and UK, the Convention People's Party (CPP) campaigned for independence with the slogan "Forward ever, backward never" and a series of strikes and boycotts. As part of a movement of Pan-African thinkers who believed that "independence is meaningless unless it is linked up with the total liberation of Africa,"[111] Nkrumah was a staunch socialist who also organized the All-Africans Peoples' Conference (AAPC) in 1958, an event that led to the birth of the Organization of African Unity (OAU) and a cascading triumph of African independence.

It was understood then by many people involved in the independence movement that formal separation was the final obstacle to freedom. Nkrumah's 1965 book *Neo-Colonialism: The Last Stage of Imperialism* was a not-so-subtle nod to Lenin's imperialism, the highest stage of capitalism. Nkrumah argued that "The essence of neo-colonialism is that the State which is subject to it is, in theory, independent and has all the outward trappings of international sovereignty. In reality its economic system and thus its political policy is directed from outside."[112] Architecture and its role in economic sovereignty was an essential pillar in countering the neocolonial threat. When Nkrumah became leader, he scrapped the existing colonial development plan with a one-million-pound budget and introduced a 5-year approach

"There are moments in history when the consensus is that everything will change, and then things do not."

with a 120-million-pound allocation to build the Kumasi College of Technology, along with roads, bridges, harbors, and free compulsory primary education. Eventually renamed Kwame Nkrumah University of Science and Technology (KNUST), the school bred a generation of Ghanaian architects who were supported by Eastern European designers and engineers in the rebuilding of the country.

Next door in Nigeria, a political revolution was also underway, albeit without the socialist values underpinning the Ghanaian revolution or a real consensus on leadership. By 1960, it was declared an independent republic with Abubakar Tafawa Balewa as the first prime minister. Nnamdi Azikiwe became the country's first president in 1963. Architectural historian Hannah Le Roux noted, "Independence had been achieved through a fragile consensus of a spectrum of political parties which (unofficially) represented Northern, Igbo and Yoruba interests. In the following two years, a realignment of parties created tensions which came to the head in 1965 with attacks between rival groups."[113] What followed was a military coup that saw the Nigerian prime minister, the minister of finance, and numerous senior politicians and army officers executed, the Nigerian Civil War (1967–70) between Nigeria and the Republic of Biafra, and massive displacement and famine in the region. The architectural program was also a mixed affair as plans to build and expand schools and universities were paused, but a wave of the first local graduates in architecture qualified in the early 1960s from the University of Ibadan, which had been upgraded to a full-fledged independent university in 1962 to address a shortage in technical staff as "opportunities for entrepreneurial activity resulted in an emergent class of clients for architects."[114] As the government unraveled, corporate organizations constructed skyscrapers like the Cocoa House (1965), once the tallest building in West Africa.

The evolution of Nkrumah's vision was not without hurdles. By 1964, faced with growing resentment and afraid of internal opposition, he pushed a constitutional amendment that made Ghana a one-party (CPP) state with Nkrumah as president for life. Though publicly committed to a nonalignment strategy throughout the Cold War, a perceived proximity to the Soviet Union and growing unpopularity due to crackdowns on dissent, Nkrumah was exiled by a military coup in 1966. With less than a decade to realize his Pan-African utopia and undo nearly a century of formal colonization, some of Nkrumah's most significant achievements were the architectural constructions of Black Star Square (1961) and the the Parliament of House of Ghana (1965). He implemented planning projects and mass housing that were experimental in nature: two large engineering projects to harness hydroelectricity; a block of junior staff housing by the ministry of works. And, most relevant here, the construction of the College of Technology in Kumasi where a new wave of Ghanaian students would be trained, paving the way for the African architects we see today in the public realm across the world.

TROPICAL MODERNISM AND THE WHITE SAVIOR COMPLEX

In the transitional period between colonial living and postcolonial life, there was also a shift in the structures that were built. Most famously, this is when tropical modernism took root in West Africa. As a movement, it incorporated environmental factors (namely the tropical climate of West Africa) in the design and employed architectural technology to resolve some of the challenges that humidity and high temperatures can cause. The previous European built architecture, where the designs of local European countries were transplanted to foreign lands, were replaced with verandas, baroque ornamentation, and geometric forms of concrete, steel, and glass. But the school of tropical modernism was almost entirely led by white architects who were trying to alleviate African problems while omitting African culture and traditions. As with many that came before them in a variety of disciplines, from medicine to finance, the belief was that Africa, despite its wealth of traditions and materials, had little to offer to an architectural cannon that prioritized the white vision of Africa over local understanding.

Maxwell Fry and Jane Drew of London-based architecture firm Fry, Drew and Partners were particularly active in this period. To begin with there was the pre-1955 early tropical work where they engaged in the "Ghana Schools project," a series of schools and teacher-training colleges, one of which was the extension of the Mfantsipim School, the first collegiate school in the Gold Coast. Following this was the mid-tropical period (1955–1960s), when the West African University College at Ibadan was erected with an enormous grille of concrete and fly gauze to protect the building from heat and insects. According to Fry, the design was so effective that "visiting Americans ask what kind of air-conditioning is being used."[115] At the same time, they were engaged in lucrative projects in Lagos, such as the headquarters for British Petroleum and offices for the Co-operative Bank, so that by the end of the 1960s, Lagos's central business district had been almost entirely rebuilt in the style of tropical modernism.

In Nigeria, tropical modernism was also accepted by most indigenous architects as the *de facto* building mode with little thought to how Nigerian traditions may be incorporated into new structures. One of the few dissenters, Oluwole Olumuyiwa, born in Nigeria and trained in Manchester, was codirector of Africa's first architectural journal, *The West African Builder and Architect*. He saw opportunities to move away from the geometric ideal of tropical modernism to the curved molds of Yoruba mud architecture.

There is an irony to the fact that even in the postcolonial era, colonial figures were at the forefront of designing the spaces that Africans would reside in for education and work. On the one hand, this was born out of necessity—independence was required to birth indigenous African architects and it would take time to train them—but those being trained were being indoctrinated into a way of approaching architecture which largely ignored the potential of African traditions to resolve uniquely African problems. As John Lloyd, who developed the architectural program at KNUST stated in 1966: "The concept of architecture, even in its widest traditional sense, is foreign to Africa."[116] Though evidently untrue, he accidentally uncovered the single biggest issue with tropical modernism and other ideologies that are imposed on the continent but are absent of local culture—they are indeed foreign to Africa and they should not be.

We find attempts to address this imbalance in the work of John Owusu-Addo, Oluwole Olumuyiwa, Demas Nwoko, Joe Osae-Addo and Diébédo Francis Kéré that follows. Owusu-Addo, trained in the tropical modernism tradition, was able to build on his education to consider local Ghanaian culture and, importantly, the needs of local people in the designs that he led. Olumyiwa was an advocate for employing Nigerian traditions in the architectural practices of his country. Nwoko, who trained in fine art, used his outsider status to adopt a unique and rebellious approach to Nigerian buildings with Pan-Africanism as a launchpad. Osae-Addo uses 'inno-native' techniques to revitalise contemporary African architecture. Finally, Kéré's engagement with local communities helps to make his designs a collaborative process. All five men helped to make the concept of architecture relevant to Africa and its people.

John Owusu Addo: Do Not Live in a Glass House

At the age of seventy-seven, John Owusu Addo was awarded the national Order of the Volta for outstanding service to the Republic of Ghana for his achievements in architecture education. His accomplishments include cofounding the Ghana Institute of Architects, designing the iconic Unity Hall at KNUST, and being the first Ghanaian head of the architecture department at KNUST. Because Addo joined KNUST while the architecture program was under John Lloyd, he is inextricably linked to the tropical modernist movement driven by white architects. Awards are rarely handed out for one's pride in their country, but if they were, Addo would have many a statue on his shelves. Beneath all the work he did with European architects was an understanding that Africa had to wrestle back control and influence on the buildings and spaces being erected.

Born on May 30, 1928, Addo turned to architecture after reading an advert in the *Gold Coast Gazette* seeking students who were interested in reading architecture at Regent Street Polytechnic (now University of Westminster) in the UK. Before this chance moment, Addo had studied art and at the time of application (1952) was an art teacher at KNUST. After five years in London, he completed his studies and returned to Ghana in 1959, where he worked on several architectural projects with Kenneth M. Scott, a notable white architect, in Accra, Ghana's capital.

Addo was keen to build a community from the growing number of Ghanaian architects working in Accra. In 1962 he became a founding

OPPOSITE: The Cedi House office building, Ghana, designed by John Owusu Addo.

"Architects who are too lazy to consider social context are creating pastry."

member of the Ghana Institute of Architects (GIA), whose mission was to advance the architectural practice of Ghana. Its very creation was a political act in a post-independence moment, and its close ties with President Nkrumah further solidified the group's alignment with the Pan-African values and ambitions that Nkrumah embodied.

Addo was also interested in helping local populations through the practical applications of his architectural practice. As he once stated:

> "Unless the role of the architect is based on our real needs, we run the risk of running into the usual architect poses, which are similar to a jeweler creating fine adornments, very nice, very pretty buildings which are out of social context. Architects who are too lazy to consider social context are creating pastry. The architects become stars and heroes using twice as much concrete and building more for less (to reverse the slogan). What is for America and Europe, we simply cannot afford."[117]

Asuoyeboah SSNIT Flats in Kumasi, the project that Addo is best known for, is a testament to the importance he gave to living in a space. The three-story, multi-family dwellings are rectangular and square forms attached by shared corridors and walkways while still achieving privacy for each unit. Balconies and elevated yards provide a sense of privacy yet enable interaction with neighbors.

Both the formation of the GIA and Addo's commitment to local communities indicates an interest in architecture that went beyond the practice into territories of social value. There can be conflict as a Black designer between wanting your work to stand alone and recognizing that while racial tensions continue to exist, the separation is not always possible. For Addo, when you look closely at his actions and the influences behind his work, being Ghanaian was more central than any loyalty to tropical modernism. His practice reveals a dialogue between traditional and tropical principles and the need to consider social traditions in architecture, as seen in the heavy influence of Akan culture, in which the courtyard is traditionally the main family space where washing, drying, pounding of fufu, and open-air cooking occurs. Architect and academic Farouk Kwaning put this approach beautifully: "Owusu Addo believes in the sociological influence of design, functional linkages in buildings . . . Generally he is an ardent advocate of being 'truthful' to the tropical environmental context—both tangible and intangible."[118]

"Always remember that you were a Ghanaian before you became an architect. No matter how diverse the influences along the way, be guided by these three aspects of life: the sustainable, the communal, and the cultural. They mark the true path of the African," states Addo.[119] In the way that the big, tropical modernist buildings dominated at the time, so does the narrative that the movement was the spine from which all work was created, once again diminishing the local culture and the "Africanness" to a sideshow. Addo's words and designs force the questions of heritage to the forefront. The era following independence was so politically charged, it seems odd that for a long time thinking has been focused largely on the tropical modernism parachuted in by white architects and not on the intention and philosophies of their African peers.

Awards are wonderful things—Addo deserves every single one he has received—though his attempts to position Africa and its architects as central to a new, hopeful postcolonial era deserves acclaim as well. Looking at Addo's practice as "Africa first" does not distract from the architectural work he completed. It instead allows us to see his life's passage for what it was—his true path as an African.

Design Institutions as Changemakers

Within the framework of tropical modernism, Oluwole Olumuyiwa fits in neatly. The Crusader House in Lagos, a commercial development with a façade that hid air conditioning units along external shelves, is typical of tropical modernism's preoccupation with climate. Architecture House, his home and office, had outdoor living areas and a swimming pool, both motifs of tropical architecture in their reference to cross ventilation and water. Hannah Le Roux states: "In terms of these approaches, Olumuyiwa is close to the position of his colonial predecessors, including Fry and Drew and the Architects' Co-Partnership, in deriving a regional architecture from modernism through attention to climate."[120] To add to his reputation as a stalwart of tropical modernism, Olumuyiwa asserted that Nigerian architecture did not have a clear style like those of Japan, Spain, or Switzerland.

But during this postcolonial era of architecture, there was more at play than simply what was made. The contribution of architects of this time included actions beyond the assumed lane of their discipline. When infrastructure and systems were built to address years of oppression, Olumuyiwa's design practice, though aligned with the prescribed tenets of tropical modernism, was charged with an immense effort to advance the position of Nigerian and African architects in public and private building projects within Nigeria.

When Oluwole Olumuyiwa returned to Nigeria in 1958, he was fully certified and immersed in European architecture, which he had studied

OPPOSITE: Oluwole Olumuyiwa in Crusader House, a multistory commercial building in Lagos, Nigeria, which he designed, c. 1960.

Commonwealth Conference, 1960. Delegates
outside the RIBA headquarters, London. In the
middle stands Oluwole Olumuyiwa.

along with city planning at the University of Manchester in the UK. He had also completed four years of apprenticeships in London, Rotterdam, and Switzerland, among others. The typical next step for an African architect of his generation with Western training would have been to join a European practice to work on their African projects. Instead, Olumuyiwa set up his own practice in Lagos, Oluwole Olumuyiwa and Associates. Also in 1960, he formed the Nigerian Institute of Architects (NIA), as "an association of independent professional architects with the aims and objectives of fostering friendship amongst members, catering for their welfare and establish[ing] mutual support and cooperation amongst them."[121]

In his work for the NIA, Olumuyiwa advocated for all Nigerian architects and negotiated for a process whereby they would be engaged by public and Nigerian-owned institutions rather than the default option of European architects. By 1970, it became mandatory for all architectural firms to include Nigerians as partners or directors. In effect, Olumuyiwa was engaging in organized structural change that would ensure the participation of indigenous Nigerians in the architectural progress and lucrative contracts that came from the decolonization of Nigeria. In 1964, he was Nigeria's delegate to the CAA (Commonwealth Association of Architects) conference and was eventually elected to serve as it president from 1976 to 1979. In 1981 Olumuyiwa became one of the founders of the African Union of Architects.

The job of organizing, advocating, and acting as a role model is exactly that, a job. The African Union of Architects was not alone in doing this after Nigerian independence, but Olumuyiwa's record is of someone who was notably active. What was the weight of that responsibility? What kind of practice might he have had without the dual job of changing how Nigerian architects were seen and engaged with? I hesitate to label it a burden, but all too often there is hidden work as a Black professional in design, and especially as an architect where accreditation, entry costs, and closed networks make entry difficult and independence even harder. At a time when a whole country was trying to reset a system of colonization, this "work" could be seen as something to admire. Olumuyiwa's white peers did not have to (or chose not to) concern themselves with advocating for African architecture to be inclusive for African architects. Instead, this was left to the very people who had suffered from the oppressive structures in the first place.

The specificity of this moment and the surge of organizations and legislation that sprang up to meet the political transformation is what makes it a good illustration of the multiple hats that Black architects have had to wear. That there is little evidence of white European architects evolving architectural systems to match the shift in national independence is consistent with the way things operate now. A survey conducted by *Architects' Journal* showed that "the profession has a serious and seemingly worsening problem with racism, creating obstacles at every level for those from a non-white background," with one respondent recommending that "[We] need to move beyond tick-boxing and seminars with all the BAME people attending at RIBA but few white decision makers [doing so]. This isn't just a BAME problem to fix. The white people have to be in the room and held accountable."[122]

After the Black Lives Matter protests, quotes on how to be anti-racist proliferated on Instagram and books on how to be anti-racist flew off the shelves, yet anti-racist organizing in architecture—outside of the multiple groups of color who engage consistently—was mostly reduced to working groups and pledges of commitment. Anecdotally, Black architects have remarked how a post-BLM surge of invites to join panels has waned over time. For white architects and other white professionals in the sector who are still inclined to create a more just, accessible, and healthier space where Black colleagues and Black-led architecture firms can thrive, it may be worth learning more about how Black architects employed structural tools to mobilize when they were isolated and marginalized at a pivotal moment in history. Olumuyiwa and his allies made it mandatory for all architectural firms to include Nigerians as partners or directors. What would it look like if Western firms employed the same strategy with Black architects now?

Demas Nwoko:
A Maverick

Natural Synthesis was the intellectual spine of the Zaria Art Society, formed in 1958 by Demas Nwoko and other students of the Nigerian College of Arts, Science and Technology. The theory served as an alternative approach that presented Black creativity as having one foot in reviving African culture and another in using external influences—pressures that may previously have been oppressive—as instruments of advancement. Other members of the collective successfully applied the thinking to art and literature, but Nwoko used Natural Synthesis to redefine African architecture.

"I am the rebel; I didn't become it by accident," said Nwoko. "Everything I've done, I've done it deliberately."[123] Most of the maverick stories we hear rarely begin with any true philosophical roots: Richard Branson started a record label after failing to sell Christmas trees; Zuckerberg tumbled out of college and landed in a pile of billions after time spent building a tool that ranked the hotness of campus women. Black people are not immune to these hollow, mythical tales (Jay-Z and his circuitous detour to becoming a billionaire mogul via a stint selling drugs is a favourite). What these Hollywood arcs lack are the radical thinking that Nwoko's philosophy embodied. Nwoko and his community sought to bend the future into a shape that embraced elements of Africa that had been buried. In this new reality, local culture dominated, and Africa was resplendent.

OPPOSITE: Demas Nwoko was commissioned in 1970 to design the Dominican Institute in Ibadan, Nigeria. Nwoko used locally sourced materials for the building's construction.

Born in Nigeria in 1935, Nwoko could have been a part of the generation of architects who, backed by government funding, studied abroad and immersed themselves in the teachings of European architecture, then eventually returned to practice in their native country, sometimes incorporating local traditions into their work, sometimes not, mostly working on government and public projects led by white architects. But after an apprenticeship as a draftsman in the public works department, Nwoko took a different path. "Other government-sponsored students came back to work in an office. I wouldn't be studying my own idea of architecture," Nwoko said of his change of direction.[124] Instead, as mentioned earlier, he studied fine art at the Nigerian College of Arts, Science and Technology, where he formed the Zaria Art Society with Uche Okeke, Simon Okeke, Bruce Onobrakpeya, and others—all key figures in the modernist art movement in Nigeria. While most of their teachers at the college were British and taught Western art philosophy and techniques, the collective believed in the study of Nigerian artistic heritage as the center of their arts curriculum.

At the time the collective was formed, Nigeria was on the cusp of independence and the Zaria Art Society was part of the national resistance to colonization. The society's manifesto, drawn up by their leader Uche Okeke in 1960, was a poetic mixture of bold and abstract goals—"Okolobia's sons shall learn to live from father's failing; blending diverse culture types, the cream of native kind adaptable alien type; the dawn of an age—the season of salvation"—with accessible ideas— "Our new society calls for a synthesis of old and new, of functional art and art for its own sake"[125]—to create the theory of Natural Synthesis.

When Nwoko received a scholarship from the Congress for Cultural Freedom in 1962 to study in Paris, Nigeria had been independent for two years. He reappeared at the University of Ibadan in 1963 to help launch the School of Drama. The return also marked his first building project, the construction of his private residence and arts space that would evolve into the New Culture Studios for Arts and Design, a community arts institution, in 1995.

"Demas Nwoko's architectural resolution of Natural Synthesis sought to place modernity beyond the ethnocentric confines of a purely European narrative," wrote Giles Omezi.[126] With the New Culture Studios for Arts and Design, the theory of Natural Synthesis was given practical application through "New Culture," a phrase Nwoko coined that envisioned Natural Synthesis influencing "Theatre, Sculpture, dance, painting, furniture, product design and architecture; the totality of cultural production."[127] The materiality of the building reflected this approach with new block work that combined cement with sand and laterite to form a stronger hybrid local material he called "Latcrete."

The Dominican Chapel Nwoko designed in 1970 demonstrated similar ingenuity in its expression of Natural Synthesis. Commissioned by the Dominican Order, one of the largest Roman Catholic orders in the world, and situated in the sacred Yoruba town of Ibadan, the space needed to embody African traditions. The tower stands prominently as part of the chapel and is supported by timber columns and metalwork designed by Nwoko and individually handcrafted. Other buildings on the compound are arranged in a courtyard system to evoke traditional Yoruba architecture where buildings are arranged around the courtyard for protection. His other architectural works—including the Oba Akenzua Cultural Centre, his private home and studio in Idumuje-Ugboko, Bishop's Court in Issele-Uku, and the Benedictine Monastery in Ewu—are all infused with this same blend of local materials and modernist thinking.

Nwoko, along with the other West-African architects of this era, was responding to a radical structural shift with the transition to independence. Like others, Nwoko answered not just with his buildings and all the local cultural elements they embodied, but with something large and formative that could change the way Africa engaged with design. As he stated in 2005, forty years after Nigeria's independence:

> "Culturally and therefore in all things, Africa has drifted along for too long a time to the tune of the whole world not caring to have an identity locus as every other people of the world exist on. We are dwarfed and are now an embarrassment to the world. For self-dignity, we should now cloth our exposed body with the garb of our God given cultural identity to settle down as one, recognizable peoples of the world."[128]

His pursuit of Natural Synthesis and the New Culture that it birthed was meant to provide a workable ideology to fix what he perceived as a crisis of self-identity. Today, Demas Nwoko is eighty-seven years old and can bear witness to a new era of African architecture that has absorbed his teachings intentionally or otherwise and replied as a bold movement where locality and modernity are constantly in dialogue with Natural Synthesis as the unspoken heartbeat. As an architect and thinker, his response to a status quo that reduced the importance of Blackness was to find structure and credibility in African culture and manifest those values in buildings and theory. The strength in combining ideas and material work is that together they become irrefutable. As a blueprint for mavericks everywhere, especially those who seek to change the tide of discrimination and oppression, Nwoko's work should be held in high esteem.

Joe Osae-Addo and Responding to a Patronized Africa

Patronizing or disparaging Africa has been a casual pastime in the West for an unfathomably long time. It is still impossible to watch a film on a British Airways flight without several young, brown faces staring at you from the small screen saying thank you for your potential donation to a BA-funded charity that feeds, schools, or provides healthcare for them. The significance of this is that Africans are nearly always presented publicly as dependent on white Europeans to help them escape the destitution of living in Africa. In a 2018 White House meeting on Haitian and African immigrants, Trump allegedly asked why America would want immigrants from "all these shithole countries."[129] More recently, the British government, in a cynical bid to win votes, announced that it was sending refugees to Rwanda. Parking the inherent awfulness of the policy and Rwandan human rights violations for a second, there's another message to note here, which is that the UK can't be bothered to deal with this issue so they'll dump the problem on Africa because Africa is a place where things can be discarded. The outcry from liberal commentators on the awfulness of being sent to Africa is equally troubling in how it frames a return to Africa as the ultimate hell.

Architecture is no stranger to these condescending patterns. The Ghanaian architect Joe Osae-Addo compares the "stranglehold of contemporary Architecture critique of contemporary Architecture in Africa" to the eagerness to negatively report on "the post-war vilification of Africa's Freedom fighters from Lumumba Savimbi, to Kwame

OPPOSITE: The porch outside Joe Osae-Addo's house. Slatted wooden screens give privacy and break up the rain that hits the house from the southwest.

Architecture 151

Nkrumah and more recently Mugabe and Gaddafi."[130] It is suggested that to follow the Western Architectural Press is to be led to believe there are only 2 or 3 decent architects in Africa.[131] In this book's section on fashion, we see this arrogance in the form of white designers co-opting traditional Ankara prints without knowing anything about the history or culture behind the fabric. In architecture, contemporary African designers have been ignored for too long, especially with a global discourse concentrated on the need for African shelter as opposed to design. Addo and a number of his contemporaries are working to change the script.

Activism has always been present throughout the arc of Osae-Addo's career. He made the decision to move to Los Angeles in 1988 because the weather reminded him of Accra.[132] There he took a job with Bernard Zimmerman, the influential California mid-century architect and educator, that would prove to be transformative. Osae-Addo recalls Zimmerman as an activist architect who believed, like him, that the purpose of architecture was to change the world. With Zimmerman as Osae-Addo's mentor, they worked together to launch the A+D Museum and *New Blood / 101*, a 1998 traveling exhibit that highlighted emerging LA designers who have "received little attention in the media or have been overlooked in favor of the more famous 'names' for whom they work."[133] Originally from Ghana but trained in London and LA, it wasn't until 2000 when Osae-Addo was thirty-nine that he would start to think of how his work with Zimmerman could be applicable to his hometown. "There was an atmosphere of optimism and euphoria, and I wanted to be part of it,"[134] he says of this time when he visited Ghana. Elsewhere, he acknowledges that "Advocacy is a big part of my life . . . no matter what you do . . . ultimately, it's for the people."[135]

His firm Constructs LLC, set up in Accra and Tamale in Ghana in 2005, was the bedrock for what has proven to be a career spawning new buildings, design materials, organizations, and talent. The precursor to this bustling activity was his "inno-native" (Osae-Addo's term) house built in 2004 with local materials of timber and adobe mud blocks. A "no air-conditioning" policy was made feasible in the hot Ghanaian climate with floor-to-ceiling jalousie windows and under floor-breeze created by raising the building three feet off the ground. "There are no internal corridors," Addo explained, "so rooms extend from one wall to the opposite wall, allowing for free flow of light and air."[136]

Local materials received a similar level of attention once Osae-Addo discovered that scientists at the Building and Road Research Institute (BRRI) in Kumasi had developed a form of Pozzolana cement using a mix of materials that included local clays and palm kernel shells, providing an environmentally friendly replacement to more expensive, imported

"Advocacy is a big part of my life... no matter what you do... ultimately, it's for the people."

cements. In 2013, Constructs LLC partnered with PMC Global Inc. in California to acquire the rights to commercialize the Pozzolana mixture: "The ingredients of the mud hut are now available for the commercial market and the mud-hut has been reborn through Pozzoghana Limited and BRRI's hard work for its success has just begun and will be dependent on all of us believing in our home-grown industries, there should be no excuses, Pozzoghana was developed by us and should be used by us. It is the people's cement," declared Addo.[137]

The push for community with its sense of building from within is echoed in ArchiAfrika, an organization founded and chaired by Osae-Addo along with a group of African architects who believe "that economic development in Africa can be sustainable, inclusive and socially relevant."[138] In their work with local and diasporic designers, the institution looks to the continent for design solutions that consider the social identity and local resources of African cities when attempting to resolve the unique challenges that Africa faces environmentally, economically, and structurally. Their work takes the proverbial wisdom: *Give a man a fish, and you feed him for a day. Teach a man to fish, and you feed him for a lifetime.* This proverb is often evoked when discussing the needs of Africa, and begs questions about the provenance of the fish, whether fishing is really what's needed at all, and most importantly, who is teaching?

Now You See Me

The ArchiAfrika Pavilion, Venice, designed by
architectural studio Msoma Architects and
inspired by Jamestown Café in Accra, Ghana.
ArchiAfrika aims to give a platform to emerging
architects from Africa and the diaspora. It's
Chairman Joe Osae-Addo presented the opening
ceremony of the Pavilion in July 2021.

Osae-Addo opened the ArchiAfrika Pavilion at the European Cultural Centre's *Time Space Existence* exhibition at Giardini della Marinaressa in Venice. Running in parallel to the Biennale Architettura, the pavilion, developed by Osae-Addo, was designed by Msoma Architects (formerly Studio NYALI), a London-based architecture practice whose work seeks to "reflect cultural identities architecturally and spatially."[139] The final structure was a collaboration with 121 Collective, a community-led group of makers and architects also in London. Against the backdrop of a space inspired by Osae-Addo's Jamestown Cafe in Accra, the pavilion played host to four exhibitions, the subjects of which spoke directly to the issue of Western solutions being imposed on distinctly African problems.

Beginning with *The Course of Empire: A Compound House Typology* exhibit by Msoma Architects, work was presented on how the compound house might work as a response to resolving issues of urban growth. If you have been to any African city, you'll recognize the structure that Msoma Architects, is exploring here. There is almost always a central compound space and a veranda, a mix of the public and private and the semi-public and semi-private where large families of different ages and requirements often live together. The layered approach to exposure reflects the networks of relationships and cultural traditions between the residents. Rather than mimicking Western housing projects, by revisiting these original examples of the collective settlement type, the studio began to evolve the design to fit modern needs in Africa where high-density housing is required.

An equally disruptive moment in the pavilion was the reimagining of the *New Blood / 101* exhibition that had taken place in LA in the 1990s. In this version, Osae-Addo presented eleven architects who he viewed as representative of the next generation of African architecture. The selected designers ranged in location and specialism: James Inedu-George, founding partner of Hub City Ltd, which focuses on megacities; Valerie Mavoungou, who leads Atelier Tropical, a studio that employs minimalism and African aesthetics; Kobina Banning, the leader of a Ghana-based nonprofit that works collaboratively with other designers to resolve contemporary urban issues; Korantemaa Larbi, a New York–based practitioner and founder of *Design 233* magazine, which showcases African creatives who "instigate positive change through design and art"[140] and Maxwell Mutanda, Hermann Kamte, Frank Amankwah, Mokena Makeka, Charles Quartey, Kofi Adomako, and Dahlia Roberts Nduom.

By presenting an alternative vision to the Western solutions we've been accustomed to, as well as identifying individuals who might deliver on this new idea, Osae-Addo is piecing together a new reality where Africans take control of their cities and the continent's challenges—accomplished not with a vague promise of fish but with smart, considered design.

AFRICA'S ARCHITECTURAL STAR

The perceived naivety when it comes to African populations and architecture—the sense that relentless poverty and political unrest means that people are just trying to get by with a roof over their heads—has historically had a deleterious effect on how African architects are regarded. Regardless of where they trained, there's sometimes been a lingering sense that these architects are somehow unsophisticated. Where this has begun to change starts with Sir David Adjaye. Born in Tanzania and of Ghanaian heritage, Adjaye was one of the first to gain recognition for his work and practice, and his reputation has gone a long way in altering perceptions of what an African architect is capable of. His body of work includes private homes for creative juggernauts like Jake Chapman, Jurgen Teller, and Chris Ofili as well as the National Museum of African American History and Culture in Washington, D.C., and the Stephen Lawrence Centre built in memory of the Black teenage architect student murdered in the UK. Mostly, Adjaye's buildings were not developed in Africa—the knighthood and adulation was the result of the buildings he designed across the UK and US. But more recently, with Adjaye's Ghana Freedom Pavilion at the Venice Biennale in 2019 and his work on the National Cathedral of Ghana in 2018, his prestige is drawing international attention to Ghana's wider cultural and creative energy, beyond the brilliance of Adjaye's work.

Adjaye's Ghana Freedom Pavilion, at the 58th Venice Biennale, was Ghana's first at the prestigious biennale. Named after the E.T. Mensah song written on the eve of Ghanaian independence, renowned artists El Anatsui, Ibrahim Mahama, Felicia Abban, Lynette Yiadom-Boakye, John Akomfrah, and Selasi Awusi Sosu all showed work interrogating the legacies of Ghana's freedom within the pavilion. The National Cathedral of Ghana, once completed, will be momentous as the first religious space for events like state funerals and inaugurations. It will also house Africa's first Bible Museum and Documentation Center, where the importance of Africans within the text will be investigated.

Placing Ghanaian architecture within the context of the Venice Biennale and building cathedrals achieves ends similar to Osae-Addo's goals. Raising the profile of new African architects and showcasing the possibilities of local materials and ideas are part of a wider movement where Africans are shifting stale perceptions and tired tropes about what Africa is and what it and its people deserve. The same can be seen in the international regard given to African literature in the recent past or with the rise of Afrobeats. Ghana's Year of Return in 2019, marking 400 years since enslaved Africans touched down in America, was an example of genius marketing meeting a renewed sense that Africa is home to opportunity for the global African diaspora. Importantly, this international interest in Africa is not the end goal, but simply the by product. This is significant in that it definitively contradicts the pervasive story that Africa is somehow lesser intellectually and creatively than the rest of the world.

Like Adjaye, Osae-Addo's work acts as a counternarrative to Africa as victim and reframes her as empowered. By demonstrating that Africa can create and play host to exceptional architectural design and design thinking, the world is reminded that Africa is a place of resource. But more importantly, it reminds the African diaspora that they can be proud of Africa—their home.

"Osae-Addo is piecing together a new reality where Africans take control of their cities and the continent's challenges—accomplished not with a vague promise of fish but with smart, considered design."

Diébédo Francis Kéré: Building Back Africa

At just over 100,000 square miles, Burkina Faso sits landlocked in West Africa, bordered by Mali to the northwest, Niger to the northeast, Benin to the southeast, Togo and Ghana to the south, and the Ivory Coast to the southwest. Formerly a French colony, the hard-won independence of 1960 brought a period of political unrest with a cluster of coups, military interventions, and famine, eventually culminating in the rise of President Thomas Sankara in 1983. The new president implemented a series of revolutionary programs: mass vaccinations, infrastructure improvements, the expansion of women's rights, encouragement of domestic agricultural consumption, and anti-desertification projects, while renaming what was then the Republic of Upper Volta to Burkina Faso, meaning "land of the honest men" (the literal translation is "land of the upright men"). The ambitious programming also included: a far-reaching anti-imperialist agenda rejecting all foreign aid; nationalization of Burkina Faso land and mineral wealth; a national literacy campaign; land redistribution to peasants; railway and road construction; outlawing female genital mutilation, forced marriages, and polygamy; and vegetation and ecological measures to support food security. By 1987, only four years after the launch of Sankara's agenda, Burkina Faso had become food self-sufficient. That same year, Sankara and others were assassinated in a coup led by Blaise Compaoré, who then became president. He is currently on the run for the murder of Sankara while the country reverts back to a pattern of

opposite: Students sitting in the shade of Gando Primary School, Gando, Burkina Faso. The school is designed by combining traditional building techniques with modern engineering.

coups and attempted coups, placing it in the unenviable position of being in the United Nation's top ten list of least developed countries.

It's a story played on loop in West Africa: independence, hope, political unrest, a long tail of poverty and progress that moves too slowly for populations urgently needing food, housing, and education. With African governments often lacking in resource or political motivation, there is a vacuum of necessity that the African diaspora of creatives, including the designers and architects among them, is increasingly motivated to fill.

Diébédo Francis Kéré is the recent recipient of the coveted Pritzker Architecture Prize. The first African and first Black person to receive the award, Kéré has been answering the call to rebuild in Africa since the launch of the Kéré Foundation in 1998, established to advocate for a child's right to a comfortable classroom.

Born in the village of Gando, Burkina Faso, in 1965, Kéré was sent to live with his uncle in the city, as there was no school in Gando at the time. His father was the village chief and Kéré was the first child in the village to be sent to school with the intention that he would return literate, specifically to read and translate his father's letters. When he came back during holidays, local women were always keen to support his education.

> "By the end of every holiday, I had to say goodbye to the community, going from one compound to another one. All women in Gando would open their clothes like that [gestures] and give me the last penny. In my culture this is a symbol of deep affection. As a 7-year-old guy, I was impressed, I asked my mother one day, 'Why do all these women love me so much?' She just answered, 'They are contributing to pay for your education, hoping that you will be successful, and one day come back and help improve the quality of life of the community. I hope now that I was able to make my community proud through this work."[141]

The education in the city led to an opportunity in 1985 for Kéré to complete a vocational carpentry scholarship in Berlin. In 1995 another scholarship took him to the Technische Universität Berlin, where he graduated in 2004 with an advanced degree in architecture. During his studies, he began work on the Gando Primary School completed in 2001. Built with mud bricks rather than concrete because the latter is not only expensive but also ill-suited to the local hot climate, a raised tin roof both protects the brick from rain and allows air to circulate and cool. In an act demonstrating empathy and insight, Kéré engaged villagers by drawing his plans in the sand and actively listened and incorporated their suggestions and improvements, stating: "Only those

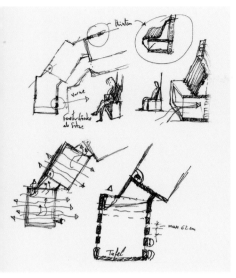

ABOVE: Detailed sketches of Lycée Schorge, Koudougou, Burkina Faso, by Francis Kéré.

RIGHT: Community members transporting clay pots to be used in the roof construction of the Gando School Library.

who are involved in the development process can appreciate the results achieved, develop them further and protect them."[142] The phrase "it takes a village" was literal here, and everyone participated while being given the opportunity to learn construction techniques on site.

The Dano Secondary School followed, largely completed by those trained in building Gando Primary. This time, laterite stone, also championed by Demas Nwoko, was the main building material. Set to an east–west orientation that reduces direct solar radiation onto the walls, with a large roof for ventilation and shade, Kéré once again responded to local climate issues using local technologies, specifically a technique where small quantities of cement combined with mud were poured into a mold, speeding up the slower brick-by-brick process utilized at Gando Primary.

If all of this material detail reminds you of Nwoko's Natural Synthesis with its blend of African culture and modern technologies, the community methods should also bring to mind some of the societal goals that John Osae-Addo was trying to achieve when he said that "no matter what you do . . . ultimately, it's for the people."[143] Kéré self-mobilized

ABOVE: Serpentine Pavillion, London, UK, designed by Francis Kéré. This project took inspiration from the great tree in his home town of Gando, Burkina Faso, where members of the community would meet to reflect on the day, 2017.

OPPOSITE: Sketch of the Serpentine Pavilion by Francis Kéré.

and created this change from the onset of his career, recognizing that his achievements were supported by his local network. "I considered my work a private task, a duty to this community. But every person can take the time to go and investigate from things that are existing. We have to fight to create the quality that we need to improve people's lives,"[144] Kéré stated upon receiving the Pritzker. There's nothing to suggest that he was talking to Black people or the African diaspora specifically, but his words may resonate strongly with this group. The act of building has long been a way of connecting with home. More recently, the urge to build something concrete, to take ownership and provide for what Africa needs, is being pursued not just by architects, but by the entire diaspora community.

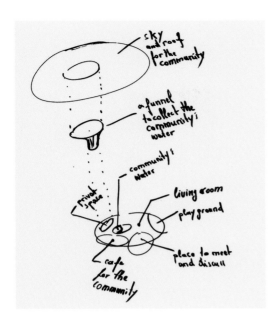

The following text labels appear in the sketch: sky and roof for the community; a funnel to collect the community's water; community's water; private space; living room; play ground; place to meet and discuss; cafe for the community

YEAR OF RETURN

It would have been hard to miss Ghana's Year of Return. There are pictures of Naomi Campbell side by side with Ghana's current president, Nana Akufo-Addo. Cardi B donned a latex version of the Ghanaian flag and Idris Elba appeared, statesman like, in conversation with President Julius Maada Bio of Sierra Leone. The website for the project calls it:

> "a major landmark spiritual and birth-right journey inviting the Global African family, home and abroad, to mark 400 years of the arrival of the first enslaved Africans in Jamestown, Virginia. The arrival of enslaved Africans marked a sordid and sad period, when our kith and kin were forcefully taken away from Africa into years of deprivation, humiliation and torture . . . 'The Year of Return, Ghana 2019' celebrates the cumulative resilience of all the victims of the Trans Atlantic Slave Trade who were scattered and displaced through the world in North America, South America, the Caribbean, Europe and Asia."[145]

In practice, it wasn't just Ghana people returned to—the diaspora found themselves all over the west coast of Africa. Another potentially unintended outcome was the magnetic pull it generated for first-generation Africans who had left to make their fortune in other lands and second-generation Africans who began to consider establishing themselves on the continent.

Interior of Gando Primary School.

Thomas Sankara Memorial, Ouagadougou,
Burkina Faso, designed by Francis Kéré to
commemorate the seminal 20th-century
Burkinabè thinker, former president and
change-maker Thomas Sankara.

Amoako Boafo, the Vienna-based, Ghana-born artist, came to hold a place in the public consciousness when his work appeared all over the Dior catwalk, courtesy of Creative Director Kim Jones in February 2021. The paintings, mostly figurative portraits radiating a quiet joy as the eyes stare at you from the canvas, were transferred to jumpers and accessories for the collaboration. Even without the Dior endorsement, Boafo was becoming a star in the art world with blue-chip gallery representation and works selling for over $1 million dollars. Amid all the hype, the quiet announcement came that Boafo would be building a studio and gallery in Ghana to nurture and support the local art scene. The Viennese architectural studio Tzou Lubroth Architekten designed a space in Accra that could act as art studio, artist residence, and gallery. Architecturally, the space is a stunning mix of curved earthiness and steel modernism. More important is the intent that it demonstrates in contributing energy to the arts culture of Ghana.

The late Virgil Abloh showed similar intention with a $380,000 donation made to Generation Unlimited, UNICEF's youth and entrepreneurship program in Ghana, by his employer Louis Vuitton. As part of the gift, Abloh led a masterclass with 250 people covering, among other things, how to become a changemaker in your community. Louis Vuitton commented at the time on Abloh's connection to Ghana driving the contribution. "A member of the Ghanaian diaspora, Virgil Abloh is devoted to making a personal contribution to help accelerate results for children and young people in Ghana. A key ambition is to inspire African youth to develop creative projects, which link African art and culture to the markets and create awareness of the Black canon."[146]

Significant efforts to commence the change Abloh advocated has come from the architectural community in the form of the African Futures Institute, whose "mission is to transform contemporary architectural education by uniting teaching, research and practice in an innovative, critical and globally relevant way. Recognising Africa's unique position as a young, dynamic and rapidly changing continent".[147] Sir David Adjaye and Professor Lesley Lokko, former director and founder of the Graduate School of Architecture at the University of Johannesburg, initiated the institute together, giving credence to the idea that building is the balm that Africa needs.

The carnage of colonization is stamped all across Africa. Architects cannot hope to erase this immediately, yet their efforts are encouraging an era where "the year of return" becomes a lifetime of building back. Kéré and his school projects are a worthy example of this movement, one that provides much needed hope. "Only inspired people are capable of having visions, and being energized to see them through,"[148] Kéré has said. And so he, along with a generation of African designers living on and off the continent, seek to inspire. It might be the very thing that turns Africa from a continent constantly hailed for its potential, to one that fulfills it.

Samuel Ross
Charlene Prempeh

Samuel Ross is a British artist, designer, and multidisciplinary creative director. He is the founder of luxury menswear brand A-COLD-WALL*, which brings together garment design, large installations, and sound design.

CP: How would you describe the current relationship between architecture and Black culture?

SR: From my perspective the relationship between Black culture and architecture seems to veer between deep comfort and otherness. This pertains to our relationship and historic dynamic, to western architecture in particular—to not dial into a subset of intellects, and to try to capture a median view, it appears to tie directly to the picture neoclassical or colonial architecture personifies.

In relation to eastern architecture, in particular traditional Japanese architecture, there seems to be a pull from our diaspora to engage with alternative architectural philosophies and histories that do not focus extensively on the notion of western dominance through tangible materials to assert a stance of power.

In addition to eastern architecture principles, what feels like a fresh introduction and link to west and east African architecture has come to the fore—a sense of self permeating through physical material, facades, and elevations has led to the distancing of western architecture and Black culture's tenuous relationship.

CP: What's the most positive change that you've seen in the past few years in the industry?

SR: Moments of collective support do occur within the sector, though association from skin tone alone remains a questionable matter of discussion.

With more inclusion occurring, it's opening up opportunity for more specifics as to why one would form or find collectives—that in itself is refreshing.

Critique among peers wishing to incorporate identity politics into commercial ventures is occurring, this signals to a maturation of net-positive expectations for those wishing to integrate commerce and ethics.

CP: When you think about the history of Black designers, what patterns, good or bad, do you see being repeated?

SR: I don't necessarily see repetition—I see at times symptomatic matters that reshape and that are reinterpreted. Possibly eternal truths or commonalties we feel are relatable, this can conjure as a reaction to difficulties such as systemic injustices, economic matters, or a sense of otherness that too often is quite frequent. The patterns of thought can also take shape in more immediate matters—through references to childhood, food, and scent.

CP: Who are the Black architects that you're most excited by now and why?

SR: Sir David Adjaye remains a constant; in relation to forming an undoubtedly Black diasporic language that expands beyond associations of struggle, he leans into the reaction to such matters versus the cause—power, intensity, volume.

Adjaye's strategic commissions are as pertinent and combative as the forms that often arise from his architectural firm. The Stephen Lawrence Centre, Smithsonian's National Museum of African American History and Culture, and Ghana's National Cathedral do well to express the notion of conscious architecture of the diaspora.

CP: What does the future hold for Black architecture globally?

SR: It's impossible to define. Optimism, choice, autonomy are aspects of Black architecture I look forward to seeing increase and take shape in the future.

Endnotes

91   Aamna Mohdin and Carmen Aguilar García, "Black people in England and Wales three times as likely to live in social housing," *The Guardian*, March 15, 2023, https://www.theguardian.com/society/2023/mar/15/census-black-britons-social-housing-ons#:~:text=While%2016%25%20of%20white%20British,backgrounds%20living%20in%20social%20housing.

92   Howard Husock, "How Progressives' Grand Plans for Subsidized Housing Have Harmed African Americans," *AEI*, November 27, 2022, https://www.aei.org/op-eds/how-progressives-grand-plans-for-subsidized-housing-have-harmed-african-americans/.

93   National Council of Architectural Registration board, "2020 NBTN Demographics," *NCARB*, May 18, 2020.

94   Architects Registration Board, *Annual Report & Financial Statement for 2020* (Architects Registration Board, 2020), p. 20.

95   "Ensenada Has New Hotel: Work Now Under Way on Old Mexico Resort Build by Prominent Business men," *Los Angeles Times*, June 5, 1927, sec. V:9.

96   K.E. Hudson, *The Will and the Way: Paul R. Williams, Architect* (Rizzoli, 1994), p. 23.

97   Paul R. Williams, "I Am a Negro," *The American Magazine*, July 1937, p. 161.

98   Ibid.

99   Emily Chen and Jenny Dorsey, "Understanding… Respectability Politics," Studio ATAO, January 7, 2021, https://www.studioatao.org/respectability-politics.

100   Paul R. Williams, "I Am a Negro," *The American Magazine*, p. 163.

101   VisionaryProjects, "Norma Sklarek: My Childhood," https://www.youtube.com/watch?v=GssFR02cx8g&t=3s.

102   Brian Lanker, *I Dream a World: Portraits of Black Women Who Changed America* (Stewart, Tabori & Chang, 1989), p. 40.

103   "Terminal One," *Architectuul*, https://architectuul.com/architecture/terminal-one#:~:text=%22At%20first%2C%20the%20architects%20working,the%20only%20one%20on%20schedule.%20.

104   Shannon Werle, "Meet Two Pioneering Women Architects," *Columbia News*, January 28, 2021.

105   Hilyard R. Robinson, "Opportunities for the Negro Architect," *Negro History Bulletin* 3, no. 7 (1940): 102–9, http://www.jstor.org/stable/44212008.

106   "Something Is Missing," HURecord, *The Howard University Record*, vol. 19, issue 8, article 1, p. 407, https://dh.howard.edu/cgi/viewcontent.cgi?article=1055&context=hurecord.

107   Max Bond, "Still Here: The Architects of Afro America: Julian Francis Abele, Hilyard Robinson, and Paul R. Williams," *Harvard Design Magazine*, (2), 1997, pp.48-53.

108   "10 Homes that Changed America: Langston Terrace Dwellings," *WTTW*, https://interactive.wttw.com/ten/homes/langston-terrace.

109   Kelly Anne Quinn, *Modern Homes: A History of Langston Terrace Dwellings, a New Deal Housing Program in Washington, DC* (University of Maryland, College Park ProQuest Dissertations Publishing, 2007).

110   Kwame Nkrumah, Speech on Independence Day: 6th March 1957, https://www.bbc.co.uk/worldservice/focusonafrica/news/story/2007/02/070129_ghana50_independence_speech.shtml.

111   Ibid.

112   Kwame Nkrumah, *Neo-Colonialism: The Last Stage of Imperialism* (International Publishers Co., Inc., 1966), p. ix.

113   Hannah Le Roux, "Modern architecture in post-colonial Ghana and Nigeria," *Architectural History*, 47, 2004, p. 368.

114   Ibid, p. 369.

115   E. Maxwell Fry, "Tropical Architecture: The development of reinforced concrete in West Africa," *West African Builder and Architect*, vol. 2, no. 2 (March/April), 1962, p. 30.

116   John Lloyd, "Ghana," in John Donat (ed.), *World Architecture 3* (Studio Vista, 1966), p. 49.

117   Max Bond and John Owusu Addo, "Aspirations," *ARENA: Architectural Association Journal 82*, 1966.

118   Farouk Kwaning, *Professor John Owusu Addo: Modernization of the Ghanaian Tropics, KNUST: A Case Study of Unity Hall Residence* (Columbia University GSAPP Questions in Architectural History (QAH II), 2020), p. 5, https://issuu.com/mr.kwaning/docs/farouk_kwaning_qah2_prof._addo-_modernization_of_t.

119   Arc. Kojo Derban, "John Owusu Addo: A memoir of Ghana's architectural journey through the eyes of a pioneer Architect," *Design 233*, March 11, 2022, https://design233.com/articles/john-owusu-addo.

120   Hannah Le Roux, "Modern architecture in post-colonial Ghana and Nigeria," *Architectural History*, 47, p. 373.

121 "About," The Nigerian Institute of Architects, https://www.nia.ng/about/.

122 Richard White, "Architecture is systematically racist. So what is the profession going to do about it?", *Architects Journal*, July 23, 2020, https://www.architectsjournal.co.uk/news/architecture-is-systemically-racist-so-what-is-the-profession-going-to-do-about-it.

123 Demas Nwoko, "Demas Nwoko The Big Tree," https://www.youtube.com/watch?v=HzS7pQ-0cnA.

124 Amber Sijuwade, "A new master's house: The Architect decolonising Nigerian design," *Aljazeera*, August 10, 2020, https://www.aljazeera.com/features/2020/8/10/a-new-masters-house-the-architect-decolonising-nigerian-design.

125 Uche Okeke, *Natural synthesis*, 1960.

126 Antoni S. Folkers and Belinda A. C. van Buiten, *Modern Architecture in Africa: Practice Encounters with Intricate African Modernity* (Springer, 2019), p. 330.

127 Giles Omezi, "Towards a New Culture; Rethinking The African Modern – The Architecture of Demas Nwoko," *Bukka*, 2007.

128 Demas Nwoko, *The Culture Opinion* (New Culture Foundation for African Arts and Culture, 2004), p. 50.

129 Josh Dawsey, "Trump derides protections for immigrants from 'shithole' counties," *The Washington Post*, January 12, 2018, https://www.washingtonpost.com/politics/trump-attacks-protections-for-immigrants-from-shithole-countries-in-oval-office-meeting/2018/01/11/bfc0725c-f711-11e7-91af-31ac729add94_story.html.

130 Ameyaw Debrah, "Ghanaian Architect Joe Osae-Addo to showcase next generation of African Architects at Venice Architecture Biennale," *Ameyawdebrah*, August 14, 2021, https://ameyawdebrah.com/ghanaian-architect-joe-osae-addo-to-showcase-next-generation-of-african-architects-at-venice-architecture-biennale/.

131 Ibid.

132 Joe Osae-Addo, "KSM Show - Joe Osae-Addo, the founder of Jamestowns cafe, hanging out with KSM," 2017, https://www.youtube.com/watch?v=ySl07vhMEEg.

133 "School of Architecture hosts 'New Blood/101' exhibit," *Yale Bulletin & Calendar*, http://archives.news.yale.edu/ybc/v27.n4.news.07.html.

134 Joann Gonchar, "Joe Addo," *Architectural Record*, 2008, p. 118.

135 Joe Osae-Addo, "The KSM Show - Joe Osae-Addo, founder of the Jamestown cafe, hanging out with KSM."

136 Frances Anderton, "An Inno-native Approach," *Dwell*, January 6, 2009, https://www.dwell.com/article/an-inno-native-approach-adefecc6.

137 Joe Osae-Addo, "Why Abandon the Mud Hut," *Archidatum*, May 4, 2015, https://www.archidatum.com//articles/why-abandon-the-mud-hut-joe-osae-addo-and-affiliations-of-tamale/.

138 "About," ArchiAfrika, https://www.archiafrika.com/about.

139 "About," Msoma Architects, https://msoma.co.uk/about/.

140 "About," Design 233, https://www.design233.com/about.

141 Diébédo Francis Kéré, "Diébédo Francis Kéré: How to build with clay and community," December 10, 2013, https://www.youtube.com/watch?v=MD23gIIr52Y.

142 "Gando Primary School," *Architecture in Development*, https://architectureindevelopment.org/project/6.

143 Joe Osae-Addo, "The KSM Show - Joe Osae-Addo, founder of the Jamestown cafe, hanging out with KSM."

144 "Diébédo Francis Kéré Biography," *The Pritzker Architecture Prize*, 2022, https://www.pritzkerprize.com/laureates/diebedo-francis-kere.

145 "Year of Return," https://www.yearofreturn.com.

146 Joelle Diderich, "EXCLUSIVE: Louis Vuitton donates $380,000 to UNICEF Education Programs in Ghana," *Women's Wear Daily*, June 24, 2021, https://wwd.com/fashion-news/fashion-scoops/louis-vuitton-virgil-abloh-unicef-education-program-ghana-1234858226/.

147 African Futures Institute, https://static1.squarespace.com/static/60cf240cfe620145a981d6ba/t/60f71f2daf2abf11040a3522/1626808117102/AFI+eBrochure+%281%29.pdf.

148 "Architecture must fulfill a social purpose," Architect of the Year - Francis Kéré, August 11, 2021, https://www.youtube.com/watch?v=lyXZbT-tfoEedu%2Findiv%2Fo%2Fobriene%2Fart116%2Freadings%2Ffinal%2520okeke%2520natural%2520synthesis%2520manifesto%25201960.doc&usg=AOvVaw2ckZMATJt7k9QxL_PI2w2G.

GRAPHIC DESIGN

INTRODUCTION

Of the three disciplines we are covering in this book, graphic design is perhaps the least explored in daily writings. Even if you claim to not care about fashion, you could probably still reel off the names of a few fashion houses. If architecture isn't consciously your thing, there are probably buildings that you can identify and, on closer inspection, may even realize you love. Graphic design occupies a strangely liminal space as it is at once ubiquitous and unknown. We see the results in the advertising we consume, the graphics on T-shirts, the magazines we read, the cartoons we love, and the sweatshirts we proudly wear emblazoned with our favorite mantras, but we do not think carefully about where these signs have come from, who has developed them, or what we may not be seeing at all. This is in part because the role of graphic design appears to emphasize or refine an existing cultural artefact—the icing on the proverbial design cake—but this perception is wildly off base. Yes, graphic design can make something look good, but its most important function, its mission as I see it, is to deliver a message in a way that resonates. There is little that is more profound or essential.

The Black designers in this section grasp the substance of graphic design in the tenor of their work and the relentlessness with which they have pursued their careers. Jackie Ormes, who has taken on a "Godmother of Graphic Design" status as people have recently rediscovered her work, used her cartooning skills to convey quietly radical storytelling that denounced the racist and misogynistic views in America at the time. Charles Dawson, who also forged his career before the rise of the Civil Rights Movement, published his book the *ABCs of Great Negroes* using the enduring format of the alphabet to illuminate Black figures who deserved recognition. Analyzing the work of Emory Douglas is to witness the eviscerating and rallying capacities of word and image in a war for equality that extinguishes any lingering questions about the forces that graphic design can exert on social change. Even when the end was not always overtly political, as is the case with film poster designer Art Sims and creative agency founder Emmett McBain, their presence and success in fields where Blackness was not prevalent was a political act in itself. The work they produced, in its sensitive unpacking of Black culture, also helped to create a blueprint for a less hackneyed presentation of Black people today.

Arriving at the present, it may simply be that I need to get better at making lemonade when the world gives me lemons, because what I'm compelled by is how much further there is to go for graphic design to become a hospitable playground for Black talent. I both celebrate and despair at the fact Liz Montague is the *New Yorker*'s first Black cartoonist; I scratch my head at the absence of a Black graphic design studio to rival the giants; I am baffled by the persistently low numbers and visibility of Black people in the profession. There are more positive expressions voiced elsewhere. Of the beautifully curated *The Black Experience in Design: Identity, Expression & Reflection*, David Rice, founder and chairman of the Organization of Black Designers, applauds the "critical mass of Black designers, practicing at the highest levels of the profession," and calls *The Black Experience in Design* "a celebration of all that we have accomplished."[149] This section of *Now You See Me*, though not quite the party one might hope for, does rightly pay respect to the remarkable work being done by Black designers, but as always, the question is how do we open up the floor to more of what is clearly a great thing?

JACKIE ORMES AND THE ERASURE OF FEMALE GENIUS

When I first saw the works of Jackie Ormes, a Black cartoonist who made the majority of her creations in the 1940s and 50s, the politically charged dry humor, complimented with female characters who were both glamorous and complicated, gave me pause. Without any real deliberation, the thought passed my mind that the work, and she, were "genius." The longer the idea of genius lingered and the more I read and saw of Jackie Ormes's creations, it became apparent that the fleeting thought was actually quite loaded. The question of who gets to define genius, how and why that label is coveted, and the history of the term becomes infinitely more charged when you consider these questions in the context of the Black female and register her wholesale absence from the debate. Jackie Ormes's genius has not been examined because Black female genius is not perceived as legitimate. But I found that she and her work deserved the accolade of "a person who is unusually intelligent or artistic, or who has a very high level of skill,"[150] and that by bestowing it upon her, we can begin to address a record of genius where Black women have been expunged.

To be labeled an artistic genius is to enter a rarefied space where laymen must bow at your feet. For art and culture critics, it's the peak of hyperbole when they've run out of vocabulary to express how talented an individual is, and for academics it can be a serious, considered assertion to classify a particular quality of creative output. Unlike *good*, *bad*, *ugly*, *pretty*, *nice*, or *difficult*, *genius* is a noun. When it is used, it is not a descriptor of a person, it is simply who they are. Etymologically, genius comes from the Latin *gignere*, meaning "to give birth or bring forth."[151] It was originally believed that people had a guardian deity or spirit watching over them from birth called a genius, which gave them their unique abilities. This is partly why the mythical genius has such a hold on our collective imagination today as a godlike figure—it has always had spiritual and otherworldly connections.

In the seminal essay by Linda Nochlin, "Why Have There Been No Great Women Artists?", she connects the trail of fabled storytelling to our modern understanding of genius. "What is stressed in all these stories is the apparently miraculous, non-determined, and a-social nature of artistic achievement."[152] She points to the example of Picasso passing all his entrance exams to both the Barcelona and Madrid Academies of Art at age fifteen and tales of Filippo Lippi, Nicolas Poussin, Gustave Courbet, and Claude Monet drawing caricatures in the margins of their schoolbooks rather than studying. By imbuing genius with this godlike status, the underlying message is that genius is bestowed rather than cultivated. The influence of sexism and racism is ignored in favor of a narrative that women and Black people have missed out on genius as an accident of birth. But this is of course false. Genius is not exempt from the atrocities of discrimination; if there is one thing we must all agree on, it is that genius is not objective.

Cody Delistraty expands on Nochlin's work in his piece "The Myth of the Artistic Genius."[153] Here he highlights the masculine traits implied in those within the golden genius circle: they are "cantankerous, people-hating men," "they flout the rules, they place themselves above everyone else."[154] He goes on to discuss the absence of female geniuses in art. "Because the understanding of artistic genius has been so closely linked to privileges and traits associated with masculinity," he writes, "women have forever been locked out of the conversation."[155] This has echoes of Nochlin questioning the ideological foundations of scholarly disciplines referencing John Stuart Mill's assertion that we tend to accept whatever is as natural.[156] So, because white men have been historically positioned as geniuses, we see their traits and their achievements as what genius should be. Even when we attempt to argue that non-white, non-male visual artists have achieved these rarefied heights, we are trying to prove their genius through a framework based on the white male. "[I]n reality the white-male-position-accepted-as-natural, or the hidden 'he' as the subject of all scholarly predicates is a decided advantage, rather than merely a hindrance or a subjective distortion,"[157] writes Nochlin. "[W]e may see the unstated domination of white male subjectivity as one in a series of intellectual distortions which must be corrected in order to achieve a more adequate and accurate view of historical situations."[158]

Torchy Brown Heartbeats comic strip, 1951.

"I SEE THE
ABSENCE OF
BLACK WOMEN
IN THE CREATIVE
GENIUS CANNON
. . . AS BEING
RELATED TO
FUNDAMENTAL
ASSUMPTIONS
ABOUT WHAT
IS CLEVER, WHAT
IS IMPORTANT,
AND WHAT
IS FUNNY."

The essay goes on to argue that there have not been any great female artists and we need to be unsentimental in assessing why. Another point is that the lack of great female artists is not due to a dearth of talent. "Thus, women and their situation in the arts, as in other realms of endeavor are not a 'problem' to be viewed through the eyes of the dominant male power elite. Instead, women must conceive of themselves as potentially, if not actually, equal subjects, and must be willing to look the facts of their situation full in the face, without self-pity, or cop-outs."[159] Her logic is that genius is not in fact a form of internal magic but something that is nurtured and reinforced. Moreover, there is no inherent connection between a "genius" and their artwork: "the naïve idea that art is the direct, personal expression of individual emotional experience, a translation of personal life into visual terms. Art is almost never that, great art never is,"[160] she writes. The false connection has become fact because people write about these white men as if they—not their work—are inherently great, and they are irrefutably great because they have been written about. There is no more to it than the often-quoted Austin Powers joke, "I eat because I'm unhappy. I'm unhappy because I eat." Though Nochlin mentions the white male specifically, she is mostly preoccupied with the position of women rather than Black people. And there is certainly no discussion on the intersectionality of the Black female experience and how gender and race inequality can exacerbate each other. It's a shame this aspect isn't explored because it significantly underscores and challenges much of what Nochlin is trying to say.

Unlike Nochlin's point about there not actually being any great female artists, I see the absence of Black women in the creative genius cannon and in Jackie Ormes's case, specifically within the cartoon cannon, as being related to fundamental assumptions about what is clever, what is important, and what is funny. None of these ideas are objective. When you look at the list of great satirists, they are making work about a political elite dominated by white men with a similar perspective to their own. Is a comic about a Black woman by a Black woman any less inherently offbeat than one about Trump by an old white man? The idea that there materially haven't been any Black female geniuses in this space suggests that there is no subjectivity involved in the assessment of the work, and we know instinctively and through experience that this is not true.

This doesn't mean that Nochlin is not right to highlight that the circumstances of white 'geniuses' has positively impacted their potential to craft and hone their work. Whether it's financial stability, the opportunity to fail upwards, the availability of a well-positioned network or just the blind confidence that comes from permanently being in a position of power, the environment for development is a fertile one. But when you look across the creative spectrum at literature, music, art, fashion *and* comics, Black women have continued to make glorious work in spite of, or even because of, their circumstances. A surface assessment unveils the work of artists old and new—Maya Angelou, Bernardine Evaristo, Aretha Franklin, Lizzo, Faith Ringgold, Kara Walker, Ann Lowe, and of course, Jackie Ormes—who have all made work that stand out as independently exceptional regardless of the person that sits behind it. There is space to argue that Black women's genius has more meaning because of the very fact that it is hard won. There is also the point that negotiating hostile environments and being able to create successfully indicates a genius for survival that would be wrong to overlook. Jackie Ormes, with her scathing, intelligent sketches, made great work. As an individual who was able to navigate a professional space that was not welcoming of women or Black people, I'd argue that contrary to Nochlin's attempts to separate the individual from the art, Ormes was personally and professionally a genius.

Ormes's satire of life as a Black woman was personal, having herself lived through the jarring experience of the conflating prejudice that Black women face. Often described as "the first black woman syndicated cartoonist," Nancy Goldstein, an Ormes biographer, made the fair point that a better title would be "the first [and] only black woman cartoonist of her time,"[161] a position she held for decades. Her career began when she wrote a letter to the editor of the African American newspaper the *Pittsburgh Courier* after graduating from high school in 1930. As the arts editor for the school's yearbook she had drawn caricatures of the students and teachers. She started as a proofreader at the *Pittsburgh Courier* and proved herself enough to start writing assignments, covering boxing matches and then court cases, police beats, and human-interest topics. The paper would eventually launch her first comic strip Torchy Brown in *Dixie to Harlem* from 1937–1938.

Torchy Brown, the heroine of the comic, was a Mississippi teen who achieved fame and fortune by singing and dancing in the Cotton Club, the legendary Harlem nightclub in New York. Like many African American women at the time, her backstory was part of the Great Migration of African Americans from the rural South to the urban Northeast between 1910 and 1970. The comic adhered to the tradition of all great comedy by wrapping sensitive social commentary in high-energy slapstick, and there was much to mine when it came to adapting to life in the North, managing the traps set for Black women, and the economic trials of making it in the city. One of my favorite sketches is when Torchy realizes, in a moment of relief when a Northerner is helping her with luggage and a place to stay, that she'd actually entered into a situation where she was being put up for prostitution gigs. In another, her light skin causes confusion on the train, and she is able to sit next to an Italian with the same skin tone in the white carriage, highlighting this particular absurdity of segregation where Black people could (and did) frequently pass as white.

Patty-Jo 'n' Ginger followed, running from 1945 to 1956. Featuring a precocious, vivid, political younger sister as the speaker, and a beautiful, older sister as the fashion pinup, the sketches centered the voices of Black females. This was a time of atomic bombs dropping and Japanese retreat, and Ormes played up the laughs for an audience who needed it, but in a similar vein to Torchy Brown, it takes only a perfunctory scratching of the surface to uncover serious messages of segregation, voter apathy and other political woes, and an upending of Black female stereotypes. Unlike the mammies and maids that were depicted at the time, Ormes's heroines were often strong, independent, socially and politically aware women who strove against the odds and defied social norms. They bravely faced the challenges of the day and gave her audience a window into the Black female lives they could aspire to. Meanwhile, critics only saw a young child, a hot sister, and very little else.

Along with the cartoons, Ormes created the Patty-Jo doll in collaboration with the Terri Lee Doll company in 1947, the first African American doll to have an elaborate, luxury wardrobe. Unlike the mammy-style dolls that proliferated the market, this was a real child's doll, popular with Black and white children that now stands as a highly valued collector's item. In 1953 she joined the board of directors for Chicago's South Side Community Arts Center, where she championed social consciousness and political awareness. Investigated by the FBI after World War II for her left-wing views and focus on political issues like race, sex, environmental pollution, and humanitarian causes, the bureau found that though she was not a member of the communist party, she had been acquainted with party members and was politically involved in events considered to be Communist Party events. Ormes was also a long-standing member of the NAACP and openly encouraged supporting the organization in her cartoons. Throughout the 1950s, she also served as an officer and fundraiser for the women's auxiliary of the Chicago Urban League, a community-based civil rights organization that helps Blacks enter the economic and social mainstreams. After she passed away in 1985 in Chicago, she was posthumously inducted into the National Association of Black Journalists Hall of Fame in 2014, followed by a 2018 induction into the Will Eisner Comic Industry Award Hall of Fame as Judges' Choice.

Ormes absolutely led a life less ordinary, rich with exceptionalism and creative genius founded on values of free speech, equality, and political activism. In an interview toward the end of her life, Ormes said, "I have never liked dreamy little women who can't hold their own."[162] The label of genius may not have readily been given to Ormes during her lifetime, but she need not have feared that anyone would suggest she did not hold her own.

Hair-Lay
Charles C. Dawson
The Classic of Combing Creams
The Truly Unusual Hair Cream
Controls the most unruly hair making it smooth, glossy, soft and healthy.
MFG. BY ALMETA MFG. CO. CHICAGO
Hair-Lay

CHARLES DAWSON AND THE BLESSING AND CURſE OF THE BLACK SIDE HUSTLE

These days, it is with interest and a raised eyebrow that I read article after article about the end of ambition and the death of the side hustle. Allegedly, the time we all spent making sourdough bread and DIY-ing during the COVID-19 pandemic has reconfigured our goals and priorities, resulting in an appetite for a more relaxed life where time well spent is measured in satisfaction and meaning, not money collected or career goals achieved. Relatedly, the side hustle, once a source of pride among the diligently hard working, is being abandoned: no one wants to work one job, let alone two! Aside from (or maybe because of) the sweet irony of these articles frequently being written by journalists who must either have a side hustle or an inheritance to survive, misunderstandings abound about why people have a side hustle in the first place. For some, it may be part of a constellation of ambition where striving for more is the life force of their universe. But for many people, it is a means to an end. Put simply, people have two jobs (or more) because they need the money. There is no surprise that the "side hustle," or the more pedestrian title of "another job," is more prevalent for people from BIPOC backgrounds.[163] There is also no great reveal in highlighting that this has historically been the case—Black people have often needed to work frantically in order to survive. This trend becomes even more stark when it comes to pursuing a career in the arts; the blending of economic discrimination and other systemic failures amounts to a history of Black people not being able to pursue their art in the singular way that the profession requires.

OPPOSITE: Hair Lay advertisement designed by Charles Dawson, c. 1930.

When I learned about the work of Chicago-born Charles Dawson, the formally trained Black artist who was finally gaining some recognition for his contribution to graphic design, it was with mixed feelings that I acknowledged his professional achievements in the artistic space. His graphic design work had been singled out for praise, but the details of his explorations in fine art suggested that this was where his true passions existed. Dawson was by no means the first artist—Black or otherwise—who had to find another means to support himself, but his experience highlights an issue that does feel more heavily weighted on the Black creative: What work was never made, or career never realized, because we were preoccupied with surviving? Whether Dawson wanted a side hustle or not, great, important work came from the spaces he engaged with outside of traditional art. The *ABCs of Great Negroes*, a publication he designed, produced and self-published, was a phenomenal A–Z guide of African American and African leaders. All things withstanding, his contribution to Black culture was significant. The question is, what else could he have produced creatively if his financial needs were less pressing and his racial experience less oppressive?

The standout moments in Dawson's career—his work leading the creation of dioramas for the 1940 American Negro Exposition in Chicago ("the largest showing of the work of Negro artists ever assembled"[164]), the *ABCs of Great Negroes*, and his Black advertising work—all sprouted from an education at Tuskegee University, the second oldest historically Black college in Alabama. Studying there between 1905 and 1907, Dawson would have been indoctrinated into Principal Booker T. Washington's vision of self-reliance. In what started off as a teacher training college, before expanding to include professional studies such as veterinary medicine and mechanical engineering, Washington insisted on teaching the practical skills needed for trade. Labor was positioned as necessary and dignified and students participated in the construction of new buildings, earning money by becoming part of the workforce at Tuskegee. Graduating from this culture of Black pride and practicality, Dawson became the first Black person to attend the Art Students League of New York, where it is reported that he was "disturbed" by racism.

This might be viewed as the first racial hurdle that rerouted the course of Dawson's career. The Art Students League of New York was (and is) a magnet for brilliant artists—Georgia O'Keeffe, Jackson Pollock, Roy Lichtenstein, Norman Rockwell, Ai Weiwei, and Louise Bourgeois have all studied or taught there under the guiding principle of independence. It was originally founded in 1875 by a group of artists from the National Academy of Design in New York City who felt that the academy "was too conservative and unsympathetic to their new ideas about art."[165]

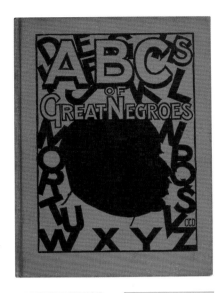

From Charles Dawson's the *ABCs of Great Negroes*, which includes hand-carved prints illustrating 26 men and women from Black history, c. 1933. Shown here are 8 illustrations along with the book cover.

What should have been a liberal hotbed was still a space that made Dawson feel uncomfortable enough to save up and move to Chicago to attend the School of the Art Institute alongside African American artist and future Harlem Renaissance legend Archibald Motley. By the time Dawson's own career began in design in 1922, he had faced the 1919 Red Summer race riots stoked by the tensions between the white working class and the growing Black community post WWI and become part of the New Negro movement to modernize culture. With advances being made by the Black population, economically and politically, Dawson completed freelance design projects for Black entrepreneurs such as banker Jesse Binga, businessman Anthony Overton, and filmmaker Oscar Micheaux, and kept the fine art candle burning by establishing the Black exhibiting group, The Chicago Art League, in 1924 with other alumni from the Art Institute of Chicago, including William Edouard Scott and William McKnight Farrow. He also cofounded Chicago's first Black arts collective, the Arts and Letters Society.

The bringing together of Black artists culminated in the 1940 American Negro Exposition, also known as the Black World's Fair. Conceived by Black real estate developer James Washington, the objective of the fair was to "promote racial understanding and good will; enlighten the world on the contributions of the Negro to civilization and make the Negro conscious of his dramatic progress since emancipation."[166] Dawson's role was to curate and oversee the development of thirty-three dioramas, hosted in the Exposition's main hall (the Court of Dioramas). Each piece was five feet wide and was hung to "illustrate the Negro's large and valuable contributions to the progress of America and the world."[167] Later, he acted as curator between 1940 and 1951 at the Museum of Negro Art and Culture at Tuskegee University.

Dawson also pursued his own practice in between these high-profile projects. In 1927, three of his paintings (*The Quadroon Madonna*, *Brother and Sister*, and *Searchlights*) were included in an exhibition of modern paintings and sculpture held at the Chicago Art Institute as part of "The Negro in Art Week." The exhibition was the first to show African American art at a major American museum. At the Century of Progress World's Fair in Chicago in 1933, he was the only African American contributor with *Negro Migration: The Exodus*, a mural for the Urban Leagues exhibit, and a poster for the Pageant of Negro Music (which is now in the collection of the MoMA). He was also one of two Black artists—the other being Archibald Motley, with whom he shared an ongoing rivalry at the Art Institute[168]—to work on the early New Deal art program that was led by the Public Works of Art Project. Ironically, Dawson was dropped after failing to demonstrate financial need.

ABOVE AND FAR RIGHT: Sweet Georgia Brown labels designed by Charles Dawson for Valmor Products, 1936.

CENTER: Perfume label designed by Charles Dawson for Valmor Products, c. 1920s.

The common thread in Dawson's work is his love for art, but arguably, his most celebrated work was in graphic design. During the Great Depression he designed "plenty of advertising featuring pleasing Negro types, my specialty,"[169] appealing to a market encouraging Black people to use hair straighteners and skin lighteners (before they became seen as the tools of oppression they are). Dawson approached the work by creating linear, flat drawings with the Black characters devoid of exaggerated racial features. As Dawson delivered these inoffensive sketches of Black male and female types, Morton and Rose Neumann, a Jewish couple who ran Valmor until it closed in the mid-1980s, refused to let him sign the pieces as his work.

When you compare the dynamic work Dawson did on the *ABCs of Great Negroes* or his role in the American Negro Exposition, the work he did in graphic design feels less like a passion project and more like a job. Contrast this with Motley, Dawson's peer, and his singular pursuit of art as his primary craft. After graduating in 1918, Motley painted modernist, jazz-influenced canvases of Black people and had early success with his 1927 piece *Mending Socks*, which was voted the most popular painting at the Newark Museum in New Jersey.[170] He was awarded the William E. Harmon Foundation Award for Distinguished Achievement Among Negroes in 1928 and became the first African American to have a one-man exhibition in New York City. In 1929, he won a Guggenheim Fellowship for those "who have demonstrated exceptional capacity for productive scholarship or exceptional creative ability in the arts"[171] and used the money to study in France for a year. More recently, the Whitney Museum paid homage to Motley in an exhibition titled "Archibald Motley: Jazz Age Modernist," and his works now sell for anywhere between $6,000 and $35,000.

Dawson's career—the successes as a curator, the quality of his graphic design, the thoughtfulness of his children's book— gives much to celebrate. Yet, there may be more to think about when reflection on his accomplishments. It is not that Dawson did not enjoy graphic design or curation or the creation of societies or writing books. The question, which is almost impossible to answer (Dawson died in 1981, so we are not privy to his perspective on the matter), is whether he would have chosen those things if the cultural landscape and economic environment for a Black man had been different then. His experience also raises important questions about the cultural landscape and economic environment now for Black creatives and how that experience differs from white people pursuing similar careers.

Where there have been attempts to address issues that Black creatives might have in sustaining themselves financially while pursuing a career in the arts, these have tended to take the form of scholarships, bursaries, one-off grants, or support in education. All of this is helpful to get people started or provide windows of financial respite. What they do not provide is the invisible safety net that allows hordes of white men with variable talent to enter the art world with no real risk, little fear, and even less distraction. A better understanding of the obstacles in pursuing creative careers and a more multifaceted, reflective approach to supporting Black creatives long term might take us away from the standard financial support models we see today into something that develops the level of confidence in oneself and disregard of failure that many white creative counterparts take for granted.

EMORY DOUGLAS AND BLACK DESIGN AS A CALL TO ACTION

It is almost impossible to look at the work of Emory Douglas without thinking of what comprised, comprises, or *should* comprise the Black aesthetic. He sits in the unusual space of straddling the Black Arts Movement—a political collective of Black creatives who adopted the Black Power movement as cultural nationalists during the 60s and 70s, calling on the creation of poetry, novels, visual arts, and theater to reflect pride in Black history and culture—and revolutionary nationalists who are best represented by the Black Panther Party. The party, where Emory Douglas was a key figure, wanted measures such as the arming of all African Americans and reparations for centuries of exploitation by white America, all built on the premise of self-defence "by any means necessary." Emory, with his blunt, provocative, sometimes violent graphic images brought the Black Panthers rhetoric to life.

Douglas's official role for the BPP was Revolutionary Artist and Minister of Culture. He oversaw the overall design of the weekly paper, which he stuffed with artworks and cartoons affirming the constitutional right to bear arms and spotlighting the cast of Black oppressors, namely police and politicians. The goal was to distil the ongoing trials of the Black community and illustrate the attacks in a way that brought clarity. In turn, that clear mindedness would ideally lead to action from protestors to bring forth their own political and social empowerment.

OPPOSITE: Emory Douglas, *November 8, 1969*. Screen print on arches paper, 100 x 64 cm (39 ²/s x 25 ¹/s in), 2009.

When you consider Douglas's inauspicious introduction to printing, it is little wonder that he funneled his design knowledge into an ongoing political outcry. At eight, Douglas moved to San Francisco from his birthplace of Grand Rapids, Michigan, in an attempt to alleviate his asthma symptoms. Five years later, he was arrested for shooting dice (a game in which players bet on the outcomes of rolling a pair of die) and was sentenced to fifteen months at the California Youth Authority in Ontario, California. There he worked in the facility's prints shop, picking up the basics of commercial printing. Later, a former counselor encouraged him to enroll in commercial art classes at the City College of San Francisco where he learned the symbiosis of art and message: "Without that foundation, I wouldn't have been able to do anything I did for the party," says Douglas.[172] At the City College of San Francisco he was a member of the Black Students' Association and designed sets for the Black poet, playwright, and essayist Amiri Baraka. Another life-changing meeting, this time with Black Panther cofounders Huey P. Newton and Bobby Seale in 1967 at the Black Panther Party Central HQ in Oakland, paved his path to Black Panther royalty when he asked if he could join the party. "We were creating a culture, a culture of resistance, a culture of defiance and self-determinatison," he says.[173] The rest, as they say, is history, only it's a history that still reverberates today when we consider the role of design and designers in a world cluttered with racial burden.

In Douglas's work as a Black Panther, design was an unconcealed path to revolution. He wanted his work to evoke enough outrage that Black people would rise up and *do* something. Unlike some of the more circuitous protests we've discussed throughout—leading by example, supporting communities, making Black lives and Black work more visible—Douglas's creative work was a direct call to arms. In this way he embodied the principles of the Black Arts Movement which were described by Addison Gayle, a key member of the movement, in his 1971 book *The Black Aesthetic* as "the serious black artist of today," in so far as they should be "at war with the American society as few have been throughout American history."[174]

Though the Black Arts Movement never claimed Emory as it's poster boy, his brand of overtly political visual protests fulfilled the criteria of the Black Art Movement's manifesto, articulated in Gayle's *The Black Aesthetic*, a collection of thirty-three essays across theory, music, poetry, drama, and fiction. Contributors from Hoyt W. Fuller, a figure in the African American intellectual culture of the 1960s and 70s, to Civil Rights activist, actor, and director Julian Mayfield ruminate on the role of Black art for Black people. Henry Louis Gates, Jr.'s description of the movement succinctly summarizes the approach:

Emory Douglas, *The Black Panther Newspaper*,
vol. 2, no. 18. Two-color ink on newsprint, 44.8 x
29.2 cm (17 5/8 x 11 1/2 in), 1969.

"DOUGLAS...
FUNNELED
HIS DESIGN
KNOWLEDGE
INTO AN
ONGOING
POLITICAL
OUTCRY."

"Defining itself against the Harlem Renaissance and deeply rooted in black cultural nationalism, the Black Arts writers imagined themselves as the artistic wing of the Black Power movement... [viewing] black art as a matter less of aesthetics than of protest; its function was to serve the political liberation of black people from white racism."[175]

In his introduction to *The Black Aesthetic*, Gayle sets the Black aesthetic up as "a corrective—a means of helping black people out of the polluted mainstream of Americanism, and offering logical, reasoned arguments as to why he should not desire to join the ranks of Norman Mailer or a William Styron . . . the black artist, due to his historical position in America at the present time, is engaged in a war with this nation that will determine the future of Black art."[176] In practice, the movement born in the late 60s was largely dead by 1975. But the book, considered the movement's aesthetic spirit guide, and Emory's work, a riot of protest, raise the same question: What is the future of Black art in a renewed wave of momentum to improve the circumstances of Black lives?

I hesitate to compare the Black Lives Matter movement to the Black Panther Party because they are miles apart in intention and makeup, but

BLM is the closest thing we currently have to a mass Black movement calling for change. Because of the differences in structure and goals, there is no equivalent Emory—no Revolutionary Artist and Minister of Culture—to pitch him against. Instead, there has and continues to be a more collective approach by various designers and creatives in the construction and content of messaging. Some messages are clear—"Stop Killing Black People" is one that has stuck—but there is no shared consensus of how we take design and use it to carve away at the messiness of racism or, more crucially, create revolution.

The impact of great poster design on the Black community is clear—who among us does not have Shepard Fairey's (incidentally a white man) iconic Barack Obama "Hope" poster forever imprinted in our minds. This vision is emblematic of a hopeful future, for many, and has since been repurposed for various demands for justice. It also contributes to what should become an ongoing dialogue on how graphic design and the mass audience it can reach may shape the future of Blackness. Emory's legacy of work for the Black Panther Party is already sealed in stone, but there's further exploration to be done on what Emory can teach us about how we can use design as a space to articulate our needs and demands and how visual consistency and repetition may be the tools to have those demands and needs met.

More recent work has already happened in this space. I was pleased when global creative studio, Fine Acts, constructed a program during the height of BLM in 2020 where twelve Black artists created twenty-four posters that were available with open access for anyone that wanted them. The intention was set for people to: "Take them to the streets. Place them around your neighborhood. Put them on your windows. Send them to friends and loved ones. Let them amplify your voice. Once again, and more than ever, it is time. To hope, and to demand. To dismantle, and to build anew."[177] The sentiment here continues to persist and yet posters and graphics as an ongoing route to resistance are yet to be employed as something to wield with rage and optimism outside of mass protest. If we were to adopt some of the rhetoric found in *The Black Aesthetic* and the Black Panther Party, we might approach the business of poster-making as Douglas did: with a laser focus on action. Graphic posters, with their succinct and accessible design, are uniquely placed to achieve this. As Douglas has stated, "I think people are drawn to my work right now because they see the same issues in it on the line today—police brutality, education, housing. It's a different time but we have the same needs."[178] What keeps me drawn to Douglas's work is the hope that his example might inspire a new type of revolution for the Black community in the vein he once sought.

It's the hottest day of the summer.
You can do nothing,
you can do something,
or you can...

DO THE
Right
Thing

Bed-Stuy

A
SPIKE LEE
JOINT

SAL'S FAMOUS Pizzeria

AM SMS
3/29/95

COPS

A 40 ACRES and A MULE FILMWORKS PRODUCTION
A SPIKE LEE JOINT "DO THE RIGHT THING" DANNY AIELLO
OSSIE DAVIS · RUBY DEE · RICHARD EDSON · GIANCARLO ESPOSITO
SPIKE LEE · BILL NUNN · JOHN TURTURRO and JOHN SAVAGE as Clifton Casting ROBI REED
Production Design WYNN THOMAS Original Music Score BILL LEE Editor BARRY ALEXANDER BROWN Photographed by ERNEST DICKERSON
Line Producer JON KILIK Co-Producer MONTY ROSS Produced, Written and Directed by SPIKE LEE A UNIVERSAL RELEASE
© 1989 UNIVERSAL CITY STUDIOS, INC.

ART SIMS AND THE CURIOUS CASE OF FILM ADVERTISING

Film posters were as ubiquitous as pot noodles when I was at university. Along with nearly every student I knew, my room was adorned with classic reprints in an affordable attempt to communicate that I was schooled in the best of popular culture and art house. As a grown woman with less inclination to prove anything, we still have movie posters up at home. They've always held a space in my creative landscape that I associate with gloss and glamour. It might simply be because they have always literally loomed large on billboards, at cinemas, in train stations, and across buses, or because of the obvious fantasy they exude, with film stars looking even more unreal than usual against the often-staged sets that don't even attempt to nod to realism. It's also because film posters seem to occupy the same space as artistic prints—they are collector's items, objects to be worshipped, the subject of nerdy forums and obscure essays, and, increasingly, an investment piece.

There are hundreds of websites dedicated to the trading of these popular objects and prestige auction houses like Sotheby's dedicate entire lots to posters. All this pomp places them more in the realm of art than advertising, and yet the designers and artists involved in their creation remain mostly anonymous. Nor is there much understanding or enquiry about how this field operates, the perceived and real barriers to taking part, or any assessment of how diverse the machine is. And yet within the industry, the significance is understood. Since 1971, the *Hollywood Reporter* has recognized the importance of entertainment posters in the launch of the Key Art Awards (key art being the industry

OPPOSITE: Poster, *Do the Right Thing*, 1989. Designed by Art Sims (American, b. 1954) for Universal Pictures (Universal City, California, USA). Offset lithograph on paper. 92.4 x 62.1 cm (36 3/8 x 24 7/16 in).

term used to describe advertising for entertainment media). Now called the Clio Entertainment Awards, the goal is still to celebrate entertainment marketing. Recently, they compiled a list of "50 Movie Posters That Changed Entertainment Marketing." Two Spike Lee posters appeared in the survey: *Jungle Fever*, which one judge called "such a gorgeous piece,"[179] pointing to the creative audacity of using just hands to advertise the film; and, *Malcom X*, was also feted by a judge for its simplicity: "The power was the power of X. Try to think of another letter that could get away with that. Not sure there is one. Who needs a title when you have an icon like this? Game-changing."[180]

The posters of Spike Lee have been iconic corner posts of cinema mania since he first gave us the luminous, graphic swirls of *She's Gotta Have It*. Like the film, the poster artwork felt fresh and funny, apart from the clichés of Black characters. Lee continued his march of poster dominance with *Do the Right Thing*, a colorful frame that, in the placement of the two main characters on opposite ends of the poster, serves up the narrative premise of the film: Who did the right thing? *Jungle Fever* and the raw symbolism of *Malcom X* take a more minimalist approach but were equally successful in drawing in an audience to contemplate the urgent messages of the films. For years, I appreciated all of this from afar without giving any real thought to how or by whom such posters were created. And then I discovered that they were designed by Art Sims.

In what seems to be the case with many Black graphic designers, Sims got his first big break in music with a summer position as an art director at Columbia Records, Los Angeles. At the time, he was studying art on a scholarship at Michigan State University after attending the prestigious Cass Technical High School in Detroit, where he grew up. In 1975, aged twenty-one, he started work at EMI and became a successful director designing music posters before setting up his own design studio, 11:24, in 1981. The numbers in the name of his studio point to the following bible verse in the *Gospel of Mark*: "Therefore I tell you, whatever you ask for in prayer, believe that you have received it, and it will be yours."[181]

And it was. The agency was not an easy thing to set up, but it was quickly a success. "It's hard to get loans," Sims recalled, "so I saved my money and worked hard to get the company in place. I did things little by little to set up my office in Los Angeles. I used CBS Studios until I wore out my welcome."[182] 11:24 worked with Spielberg on *The Color Purple* in 1985 and after seeing *She's Gotta Have It* in 1986, Sims contacted Spike Lee directly, which led to Sims working on the design for a many of his films, including *School Daze*, *Do the Right Thing*, *Malcom X*, *Mo' Better Blues*, and *Crooklyn*. "Spike was the main reason that a lot of my work got finished," Sims says "a lot of people were trying to keep me out of the business."[183]

"A LOT OF PEOPLE WERE TRYING TO KEEP ME OUT OF THE BUSINESS."

The mystique of film has long been its attraction and this particularly opaque corner of the industry has not enjoyed the level of scrutiny or change that movements such as #OscarsSoWhite has forced upon the talent and behind-the-scenes makeup of Hollywood. It is inevitably the things that are least public-facing that are slowest to change—few people are going to complain or have any awareness of the fact that there are not a significant number of Black people designing posters. What has instead been lauded are measures to improve diversity of the crew and, trumping that, the diversity of the cast and directors. But as the nineteenth-century proverb goes, "As one bad apple spoils the others, so you must show no quarter to sin or sinners." Changing an industry requires changing the *whole* industry. Film posters, with their glamour and joy, are an essential part of the ecosystem. Given the absence of stats or any real investigation into this space, and as one of the few to overcome the hurdles and make film posters that the public know and love (even if they aren't necessarily aware of the man himself!), Sims's perspective on being Black in the advertising film industry is a crucial one.

As Sims has claimed in the past, "There's a lot of African American design advertising agencies going on in the music industry, but in film and television it's very few because there is an 'old boys' network in the industry and there is a lot of racism. They have their own groups and they only like to work with their own. Very rarely is there someone that is not connected with them that is brought in from outside of their circles. In this business there is a lot of nepotism and favoritism."[184] In conversation, he tells anecdotes illustrating the absence of POC among marketing executives and is keen to highlight that this often results in the essence of the film's message being lost.

This is not a new story. Nepotism, glass ceilings, cement walls, and a plethora of barriers in various materials have long been features of other design spaces. What the case of film advertising highlights, however, is how discrimination and a lack of diversity can hide in plain sight with very little challenge or acknowledgement. Knowing who makes film posters matters because they are part of our cultural archive. We all remember the mass hysteria in the Black community when the 2018 film *Black Panther* was launched. Think pieces, articles, and social media were awash with commentary about the importance of representation, as well as discussions about the conspicuous celebration of Black culture and how the moment might affect lasting change. Costume design was unpacked, the use of Afrocentric, natural hair lauded, and of course, the majority Black cast cheered. The posters featuring large, heroic portraits of the cast were also notable for how they presented Black characters as beautiful in their entirety. Yet the main discussion about the film's artwork was whether the Chinese edition used a mask on Chadwick Boseman to hide the fact that he was Black (the jury's still out). Few would know that Art Sims was also responsible for these *Black Panther* poster designs. A hidden fact that, though unlikely to be loaded with malice, speaks volumes about the regard and scrutiny of this particular corner of the vast engine of Hollywood films.

Creative industries have long sought to address issues of discrimination and racism by first tackling the obvious spectacles of bad behavior. This might mean having brown faces in advertising or, as in film, ensuring that the cast and directors are from a range of cultures. With BLM, the behind-the-scenes issues have been more prominent, and diversity of crew has started to be addressed in film and fashion. What the brilliant work of Art Sims highlights is that the creative world is vast and sprawling and if we are to correct decades of Black oppression in these spaces, we need to actively survey and address all areas of the industry. "I love doing work for and about African Americans. I feel I am reshaping history to show our beauty."[185] Art Sims said. It's essential that a new generation of Black creatives are given the torch to do the same.

"CREATIVE INDUSTRIES HAVE LONG SOUGHT TO ADDRESS ISSUES OF DISCRIMINATION AND RACISM BY FIRST TACKLING THE OBVIOUS SPECTACLES OF BAD BEHAVIOR. THIS MIGHT MEAN HAVING BROWN FACES IN ADVERTISING OR, AS IN FILM, ENSURING THAT THE CAST AND DIRECTORS ARE FROM A RANGE OF CULTURES."

**blackball,
black book,
black boy,
black eye,
black friday,
black hand,
black heart
blackjack,
black magic,
blackmail,
black market,
black maria,
black mark,
little black sambo.**

white lies.

Black is Beautiful.

Vince Cullers Advertising, Inc.
520 North Michigan Avenue
Chicago, Illinois 60611 (312) 321-9296

EMMETT MCBAIN: MARKETING MADE FOR BLACK PEOPLE BY BLACK PEOPLE

I became fascinated by Emmett McBain when I discovered the Black Marlboro Man. When most of us think about retro Marlboro advertising, we see the iconic white cowboy, squinting at the camera in his red shirt. That image was replaced for me by one of a Black man in orange and tan standing on the street with a woman in a dotted head wrap and another of the same man buying fruit from a market. The Black Marlboro man was not a narrow-eyed, masculine trope but a relatable, everyday man for African Americans of the time. Putting aside the questionable ethics of selling tobacco, the advert opened a door to a history of Black advertising that felt authentic and respectful. The advert, made under the umbrella of Burrell-McBain, Inc. ("An Advertising Agency for the Black Consumer Market"[186]) formed in 1971, was a partnership between Tom Burrell, who was a copywriter by trade, and McBain who was a graphic designer. Burrell understood that "Black people are not dark-skinned white people,"[187] and McBain's work spoke to that intelligence with a portfolio that includes the iconic "Black is Beautiful" advert—a monochrome masterclass on insidious racism—that he made in 1968 in his position as creative director at Vince Cullers Group. The agency, founded in 1956, was the first African American full-service advertising agency.

Born in Chicago in 1935, McBain began taking weekend classes at the School of the Art Institute of Chicago when he was twelve years old. Seven years later he enrolled at the Ray-Vogue Art School and eventually graduated from the American Academy of Art in 1956 before starting work at Vince Cullers Group. Very quickly, he moved to Playboy Records as an assistant art director at the age of twenty-two, and within a year was promoted to art director. Here, he created a body of album covers for artists including Tony Martin, Max Roach, and Sarah Vaughn, winning Billboard's Album Cover of the Week for his design for *The Playboy Jazz All-Stars*. More album covers were to follow when he set up his own design studio, McBain Associates, in 1959 and worked with Mercury Records designing over seventy-five album covers by the time he was twenty-four. But it was in 1968, after returning from an extensive European and African trip, and prompted in part by fatigue with the continued racism and persecution of Black people in the US, that McBain threw himself into Black Chicago's cultural revolution and rejoined Vince Cullers to make the seminal "Black is Beautiful" advert. In 1971 he opened Burrell-McBain, designing for everyone from Marlboro to McDonald's to Coca Cola, in the process becoming the country's largest Black-owned agency. Where their work stood out was how it depicted Black people as normal and beautiful rather than exoticized. One of my personal favorites is a father and son eating their burgers in a McDonald's advert with the copy reading "Daddy and Junior Gettin' Down."

A number of factors contributed to their success at the time, but an important change taking place was that big manufacturers were realizing the value of the Black market. Prior to the 1960s, advertising to African Americans mostly took place in Black newspapers and white clients saw Black consumers as having little disposable income, as well as being dangerous by association within the politically charged climate. The realization that African Americans were spending nearly $30 billion dollars a year brought in a new era of pragmatism as clients tried to tap into the market.

It's that same pragmatism mixed with hints of social purpose and cultural relevance that drives the advertising world to speak to and include a Black audience in the campaigns it makes now. Black spending power in the US was estimated at $835 billion by McKinsey[188] in 2019, and the Black Pound Report in 2022 found that the disposable income of the multi-ethnic consumer was £4.5 billion.[189] Money aside, the cultural value of Blackness is immeasurable when you assess the impact made across music, fashion, film, and literature, among other things, giving the focus on Blackness an inevitability. Yet as someone who has worked in the advertising space for over fifteen years, what I found particularly interesting about McBain's work was how sensitive it was to the Black experience when current advertising—either featuring or speaking to Black people—seems to still struggle to hit the right note.

OPPOSITE: McDonald's advertisement, "Daddy and Junior Gettin' Down," designed by Emmett McBain, 1973.

Get Down with Something Good at McDonald's.

Daddy and Junior Gettin' Down.
Daddy and Junior really dig doing things together . . . going to a game or just ridin' 'n rappin'. But, the biggest treat is stopping for something good at McDonald's.

McDonald's

Please post this ad on your crew bulletin board.

Black marketing can be a perilous space to enter. If we split the endeavors between brands trying to discuss Black issues (where the target audience encompasses all races) and brands trying to speak specifically to Black people, it is possible to distinguish between the different pitfalls and payoffs, using some recent examples. Firstly, the now notorious Pepsi commercial featuring Kendall Jenner. At some point before April 4, 2017, a group of what I imagine were creatives, strategists, marketing executives, and client managers sat in a room and decided that it would be a good idea to draw inspiration from the story of Ieshia Evans, a Black woman who was one of 102 protesters arrested in Baton Rouge, Louisiana, in July 2016, where she was protesting the shootings of Alton Sterling and Philando Castile by police. In what has become a viral image, Evans's stance is silent before a line of armed police officers with her arms crossed, wearing a flowing dress. She was making a peaceful stand against police brutality, and she was not moving.

The Pepsi ad seemingly references this incident and the famous "Tank Man" photo from the Tiananmen Square protests in 1989. This time, a cohort of young attractive Gen Zers are holding signage with anodyne pleas such as "join the conversation" while they clap, laugh, and hug as if at a slightly less exciting version of Coachella. The film climaxes as Jenner moves toward a line of policemen and offers one a can of Pepsi. He accepts, grinning. Cue raucous applause from the crowd. If this reads as sorely tone deaf to you, you may well find the actual video astounding. Most criticism pointed to the thoughtless co-opting of the BLM movement and suggested that there were clearly no Black people in the room (or at least none that felt empowered enough to speak up). What stuck with me was the lack of weight these executives must feel for the Black struggle, that it is somehow a party or a game that is so inconsequential that the bubbles from a can of fizzy drink can right all the wrongs.

Just a year later, on the other end of the credibility spectrum where brands talk Black issues to a wide audience, is the much-lauded Colin Kaepernick commercial for Nike. Kaepernick, a professional American footballer and activist, had been protesting police brutality since 2016. First by sitting during the national anthem and then eventually by kneeling. At the point the commerical came out with Nike in September 2018, Kaepernick had not played in the NFL since New Year's Day 2017, and there was a sense that his career was being blackballed by the league because of the activism. The film saw Kaepernick narrate a story with Nike's slogan "Just Do It," with a particularly poignant moment where he suggests that one should "Believe in something even if it means sacrificing everything."[190] Though people from the "white lives matter" brigade threatened to boycott Nike, the commer-

cial won a creative Emmy and fellow sports stars Serena Williams and LeBron James offered their support. Whatever your thoughts may be on Nike as a corporate entity, it's hard to deny that this commercial was meaningful. Nike had taken a risk by aligning itself with a sportsman who had become persona non grata in his league, and what it said was that contrary to the league's behavior, standing up for what is right will be rewarded.

"BELIEVE IN SOMETHING EVEN IF IT MEANS SACRIFICING EVERYTHING."

The other mainstay of Black-marketing efforts has the primary objective of trying to get Black people to dip into their pockets. Here, there is usually a product that market research has deemed suitably compatible with the Black dollar and an advertising exercise proceeds to make said research a reality. Again, let's start with a less than tasteful example of this sort of marketing—the Puma trap party in 2018. It's been four years since this party took place and yet the incredulity that overcame me on the first reading has not waned. Puma, in collaboration with JD Sports and marketing agency Urban Nerds, threw a "House of Hustle" party where guests received Puma boxes full of £50 notes, and a burner phone that they were to use as a trap line (slang for a phone that is used for selling drugs). At the actual party, dirty mattresses were strewn across the floor—because, well, why not?—and drill acts performed, while grills were added to attendees' teeth and fresh cuts were delivered. The distastefulness of the event was called out by a number of Black people citing the effects of drugs on the Black community. One particularly eloquent letter by Amber Gilbert Coutts, a social worker based in London, pointed first to the number of murders that had taken place in London that year—"We are not even a quarter way through the year and in London alone there has been 50 fatal violent crimes."[191] Secondly, she pointed to the hypocrisy of Puma actively trying to lure a young Black audience while simultaneously being terrified by their presence. "This ode to 'the trap' in an attempt to attract the young 'road' crowd was not missed by your security team who was—disproportionately—in full force on the night,"[192] she commented. When all was said and done, Puma apologized, stating, "We want to make clear that Puma in no way endorses or intends to glamourise drug culture."[193] Well, that was a funny way of showing it.

Again, there are less egregious references to consider when marketing to a black audience. For example, the Procter & Gamble campaign "My Black Is Beautiful," which was originally started by Black women at Procter & Gamble in 2006 with a remit that it empowers, celebrates and ignites meaningful dialogue and change around the topic of bias and the ever-evolving subject of beauty, as well as its influence on culture.[194] To date, one of its most effective campaigns has been "The Talk," where Black parents have to explain to their children some of the prejudices they will face in life because of their skin color. In one commercial, a mother explains to her daughter that she is "not pretty 'for a black girl.' You are beautiful, period"[195] when her daughter relays what she thought was a compliment from a shopkeeper. In addition to the commercials, the team at P&G worked with the sitcom *Black-ish* to produce an episode about the making of "The Talk" and how to create discussion around bias through marketing. A podcast also accompanied the campaign alongside a downloadable discussion guide to help parents and other adults in an influencing position to navigate difficult conversations about bias.

Efforts from Procter & Gamble, and other brands, to fully engage with how Black people are depicted suggest that it's a good time to reflect on when this has previously been done well, and to that end, the work of Emmet McBain deserves a huge amount of attention. Even after he quit the advertising game and opened art gallery and consultancy The Black Eye, which focused on design for nonprofits and publishing houses, he organized a series of nationwide arts programms, community projects, and scholarships promoting African American voices, funded by Beefeater gin. Where brands today still stumble with clumsy representation and misplaced cultural appropriation of negative Black stereotypes, McBain focused on the very normal, very beautiful, everyday experience of Blackness in a way that spoke to and about Black people without othering. This may seem like an obvious approach, but even by the few examples provided above, it's not one that is being universally adopted.

"We've done all we can. It's out of our hands now."

JACKIE HEIRESS:
MEET LIZ MONTAGUE

When assessing the visibility of Black women in comedy, things aren't as dire as you'd expect. You have, and I say this with huge respect, the veterans—Whoopi Goldberg, LaWanda Page, Wanda Sykes—and the new guard, who are making profitable films and touring. There are prominent stand-ups like Tiffany Haddish and Gina Yashere and the genre-defining comedy *Insecure*, which shined a light on two of its stars—the live comedy of Yvonne Orji and the writing of SNL alumnus Natasha Rothwell. In the space of newspaper and magazine cartoonists, however, things get a little less colorful and a little less starry—very few people have a favorite Black cartoonist that they would be able to name or whose work they'd even be able to recognize. It holds an unusual space in so far as it's a niche creative territory with a broad reach but one that could hardly be described as popular culture. Overall, it's an industry in decline. In autumn 2022, Lee Enterprises, an Iowa-based media conglomerate with close to eighty daily newspapers, announced that they were streamlining comics. Earlier that year, News Corp Australia announced that it would drop all its comics. Yet, like Twitter, comics is a world adored by people in media and politics, and, therefore, it's a space loaded with power. And though the cake may be shrinking, the crumbs that are left are still mostly divided between a consistent cohort of white men. Given the intellectual and creative kudos of cartoons, what might we discover if we ask why?

OPPOSITE: The first comic by Liz Montague to be published in *The New Yorker*.

There is of course the wider issue that low numbers of staff journalists are people of color. The US Census Bureau shows that though racial and ethnic minorities comprise almost 40 percent of the US population, they make up less than 17 percent of newsroom staff at both print and online publications, and 13 percent of newspaper leadership.[196] Even the *New York Times*, the bastion of liberal America, was 81 percent white at the last check in 2018.[197] The structural issues that are constantly hovering are at play again: newspaper roles are low paid, cronyism runs amok through the corridors, and working internships may not be an option when you can't rely on the bank of Mom and Dad. But with cartoonists, even if they're not trying to get on staff and simply trying to get a comic published, there is the very specific hurdle of someone in power getting to decide whether or not you are funny. What one does or does not find amusing is at least in some way influenced by their own experience and context.

Let's take the submission process for *The New Yorker*, the magazine that is to cartoonists what the NBA is to basketball players. A fairly amusing submission page, written by its cartoon editor, explains how to apply, the requirements, and what is and isn't allowed. To the question of "You want to know if there's any subject matter I'm hankering for, or whether there are topics to avoid?", she answers, "Not really! I suggest you do a quick Internet search to make sure your idea is fresh, but, other than that, I'm most interested in what is tickling *you*."[198] But that can't quite be true. Here are two of the things that are currently tickling me: 1) the revival of "cold" to describe someone being mean, which is a word I used to throw around viciously in the 80s in London; 2) that my three-year-old son, who can't read yet, keeps picking up David Shrigley's book *Get Your Shit Together* while declaring, "Mummy needs this!" One of these examples is fairly specific to the culture I grew up in, which was Black and working class in East London. Contrast this with a selection of cartoons in *The New Yorker* that I'm currently reading. In the first, a quartet of Greek gods and goddesses sit on an island over a caption that reads "We might not have any worshippers, but we're still a viable intellectual property,"[199] which I read as a dig at all the nice publishers who get themselves to sleep at night by believing that the majority of the population are stupid. Another shows a middle-aged couple leaving their friend's house after dinner, captioned: "I know they should be invited to our house next, but can't we just give them the cash equivalent and call it even."[200] The inescapable fact is that both cartoons speak to a middle-class, white sensibility. I'm not saying that Black people can't find these things funny—I laughed out loud at the second one and then sent a picture of it to my husband—but they're clearly not mining anything that's from Black culture.

"A BRAIN THAT FUNCTIONS IN THE WEIRD WAY GAG CARTOONISTS' BRAINS DO—SHE'S ABLE TO STITCH TOGETHER A FUNNY DRAWING AND A SPECIFIC OBSERVATION TO ALCHEMICALLY CREATE A JOKE THAT LIVES IN A LITTLE BOX."

It all reminds me of a discussion on the subject of Monty Python I had with a dear (white) friend while on holiday that took an unexpectedly heated turn. The fumbled point I was trying to make (clumsily after one too many glasses of vinho verde) was that the humor in Monty Python was, on balance, funnier to white people than it was to Black people. I understand that this was particularly jarring as I've never even watched Monty Python, but every time someone recites the jokes, I look back blankly because it just doesn't fall within my walls of reference. Does that mean no Black people find it funny? Of course not. But it illuminates what I think is a valid issue—that what we think is good/funny/sad/right/wrong is at least partly based on our individual experiences. If then the gatekeepers in creative spaces are homogenously white, what gets through becomes not just a question of quality, but one of individual taste that cannot help but be biased toward their own experience. Suddenly, it's not that surprising that the voice of a Black woman first made it into the *New Yorker* in 2019. Her name was Liz Montague.

When Nancy Goldstein, the Jackie Ormes biographer, called Ormes "the first [and] only black woman cartoonist of her time,"[201] it read as pride coupled with exasperation. Over seventy years later, Liz Montague has become what *The New Yorker* believes is the first Black woman cartoonist to be published in its pages—after she wrote to the editor to complain about lack of representation. The cartoon appeared in March 2019 and became instantly iconic: two Black women on a rooftop flashing a signal reading "PER MY LAST E-MAIL" with the caption "We've done all we can. It's out of our hands now."[202] Montague had submitted approximately fifty cartoons before this one got published.

In an interview for the *Washington Post*,[203] it is suggested that the cartoon works on two levels. The first is understood by office workers everywhere—How many times do I need to ask you to do the thing I asked you to do in my last correspondence? The second, a nod to the fact that Black women are consistently ignored in our society on a pandemic scale. Emma Allen, *The New Yorker*'s cartoon editor, deserves some credit for responding to Montague's frustrations with an opportunity soon after she took on the role at the magazine, though it took an email spelling out the issues with representation and lack of diversity for there to be action. Notably, many of Montague's previous submissions to *The New Yorker* were rejected even though Allen sees Liz as having "a brain that functions in the weird way gag cartoonists' brains do—she's able to stitch together a funny drawing and a specific observation to alchemically create a joke that lives in a little box."[204]

Montague's contributions to *The New Yorker* are funny and tickling and illuminating in all the ways that great cartoons should be. Born in 1995 to an architect and an executive in South Jersey, New Jersey, she attended the University of Richmond on a track scholarship. In her sophomore year, a guest speaker graphic designer made her consider how art could serve as an accessible channel for communicating complex ideas. She began sketching a biographical series called "Liz at Large" that originally appeared on her Instagram account and is now a weekly cartoon in the *Washington City Paper*. *The New Yorker* success followed the year after graduation along with a cascade of other high-profile gigs, including an illustrated video for Joe Biden's presidential campaign in 2020 that was narrated by Stacey Abrams. That same year Montague illustrated a Google Doodle celebrating Jackie Ormes.

Much has changed in the world of newspaper publishing and cartoons since Jackie Ormes debuted her Black female characters in US newspapers during the 1930s, but there is still an apathy when it comes to diversity amongst the stories shared. As Montague points out in an interview, "In the cartoon world, the white male perspective is the universal perspective, and everyone else is niche,"[205] but she is also clear about trying "really hard just to stick to my perspective as an individual just because it's such a broad field of, like, black people as a whole, women as a whole."[206] She adds, "I don't want to pretend like I can represent every black person or every woman on the planet because everyone's different."[207] Hopefully no one expects that of her. What her work is providing is a window into a humor and perspective that is distinctly Black and female, and it's a relief that this particular voice slipped through the net when many others are submitting their cartoons to an audience of blank faces as confused by their jokes as I am by Monty Python. If we can agree that there are different types of funny, then we should also agree that we need different types of people as the arbiters of cartoon sketches. For publishers, this wouldn't be a worthy form of altruism, it would also make business sense as the content opens up to new audiences in a sector that is losing readers annually. "Unfortunately, the standard for people of color is that we don't get to tell our own stories," Montague has said. "I don't take that for granted. I don't take that lightly."[208] And she is right: the fact that there is nothing funny about it is something we should all agree on.

WHERE

ARE THE ➤ BLACK DESIGNERS?

JUNE 26-27, 2021
WATBD.ORG

WHERE ARE ALL THE BLACK GRAPHIC DESIGNER∫? NO, REALLY, WHERE ARE THEY?

This is less of a rhetorical question and more of a desperate call out. At A Vibe Called Tech, we are ceaselessly looking for graphic designers with a minimum level of success. I'm clearly not the only person who has noticed this as 2020 saw the establishment of Where are all the Black Designers?, a nonprofit design advocacy organization with a remit to "heal, support, amplify, and make space for the entire spectrum of Black creativity while also decolonizing design through education and wellness resources, events, partnerships, and collaborations."[209] At the moment, when you assess the major graphic design houses (Pentagram, Wolff Olins, Landor & Fitch, etc.), there is a scattering of Black people in senior positions (namely Eddie Opara, NY-based partner at Pentagram, and Forest Young, formerly global principal at Wolff Olins). If you zoom out to the wider industry, stats from the 2019 design census show that Black people make up 3 percent of the industry in the US[210] and that in the UK only 13 per cent of employees in design are from black, Asian, and minority ethnic (BAME) backgrounds (though there is no split for graphic design or Black people specifically[211]). The numbers are disheartening, but what's shocking is the picture they paint about the pace at which the design industry changes.

SAME BUT DIFFERENT

I stumbled across an article on Letterform Archive—a nonprofit center for inspiration, education, publishing, and community—that re-published

"DESIGN CAN DISRUPT THE STATUS QUO, CELEBRATE NEW VOICES, AND TELL UNTOLD STORIES. DESIGN CAN REPRESENT US ALL."

a piece by Dorothy Jackson from 1968 called "The Black Experience in Graphic Design." It details the perspectives of five Black designers working at the time and made an unusual appearance in the trade publication *Print*—unusual because it was in the midst of the Civil Rights Movement. Even more remarkable is how candid the designers were, given that they would continue working with the clients and colleagues they discussed. The concerns raised in the piece are eerily similar to what Black people face now not just in graphic design but in all professional spaces. One designer, William Wacasey, recalls arriving to keep an appointment with an art director and "having the receptionist hand me a package because she thought I was a delivery boy."[212] Now stack that up against this quote from Edward Enninful, editor of *Vogue UK*, in July 2020: "Today, I was racially profiled by a security guard whilst entering my workplace . . . I was instructed to use the loading bay. Just because our timelines and weekends are returning to normal, we cannot let the world return to how it was. Change needs to happen now."[213] Another graphic designer, Dorothy Hayes, discusses tokenism: "I was employed by a well-known broadcasting company and led to believe that I would hold a design position, yet I was never allowed to do anything but non-creative work. I was frankly told that my employment was simply a form of tokenism."[214] There are too many testimonies to compare this to, but it is fair to say that tokenism has not died in graphic design or elsewhere.

There were three additional points made by graphic designers at the time that I found particularly compelling for how they emphasised some less obvious consequences of discrimination in the industry. The first was that the graphic designers who were able to find jobs tended to stay in them. Because it was so difficult to land a role in the first place, they felt they had no choice but to remain. "Unusually long periods of employment at one job tend to hamper one's creative processes,"[215] explained Alex Walker, who had opened his own studio. "Most white designers who eventually become award-winning art directors or make lots of money spent short periods of time in various studios and agencies. With each move, their knowledge, contacts, and usually their incomes increased. This is one modus operandi that has left the black designer in the dust."[216] Again, there is little comprehensive research specifically on the job opportunities for Black designers, but statistics from McKinsey support both the idea that Black people still have fewer opportunities for work and that once employed are less likely to progress: "Black employees often don't feel that their employers value and embrace diversity, the system for evaluation and promotion is fair, and they can be their full selves. The result: a trust deficit between companies and their Black employees."[217] What both the McKinsey study and Walker's quote raise is the impact of being undermined at work because you're Black and the knock-on effect that may have on your career trajectory. In a graphic design industry where roles are scarce, it's not a leap to consider that these pains are even more heavily felt, and that talent is snuffed by the restrictions imposed. More difficult to extrapolate is what this does to a graphic designer's psyche and their ability to approach their work with confidence. How is design work affected in these current times when you are consciously or subconsciously preoccupied with being undermined?

Then there is the issue of what happens when you have had enough of a system that doesn't value you and decide to go it alone. For many, Black and otherwise, one of the main appeals of entrepreneurism is the sense that you will then be the master of your own destiny. Sadly, this optimism does not take into account the fact that as a solo agent or leader of a business, you are still operating within the original system. The bosses that underestimated you are now the client that underestimates you. The colleagues that didn't support your work become the peers that don't champion your company. In 1968, this was the case for William Wacasey, a graphic designer who had previously worked in display and lettering for retail as well as packaging and product design

The Black Experience in Graphic Design

Dorothy Hayes

William Waca

By Dorothy Jackson

Five talented black designers candidly discuss the frustrations and opportunities in a field where "flesh-colored" means pink

Original print, "The Black Design Experience in Graphic Design."

ugh
effe
tudi
ign
o th

Bill Howell

Dorothy Akubuiro

fru
eve

E
am
giv
hir
pin
exp
del

design w
to teaching
always the
n the field
he got out
ice work—
—a job w
f advertis
was afforc

Alex Walker

before setting up Wacasey Associates as New York's first Black-owned design studio. He observed that "because I was black, I tended to get the smaller jobs . . . with practically no budget."[218] In an era still feeling the reverberations of a racial reckoning, the landscape isn't hugely altered. The federal reserve released data showing that only 66.4% of BIPOC business owners receive at least a percentage of the funding requested from banks, compared to 80.2% of white business owners, and that they have $500 in outside equity when founding a start-up compared to $18,500 for white-owned start-ups.[219] VC's are similarly tight-fisted, giving away between 0.8 percent and 1.3 percent since 2017 per year to Black people as a proportion of US funding according to Crunchbase data.[220]

Let's say that you overcome the funding gap and get your graphic design business up and running. Then comes the, so far, unwinnable race to attract the blue-chip clients and match the turnover of the other big design agencies. If Wacasey Associates was the first Black-owned design studio back in 1968, then the Black-owned business to rival a Pentagram or a Wolff Olins has been at least fifty years in the making, and yet, it hasn't materialized. This is not to say that there aren't some brilliant design studios led by people of color or designers with noteworthy and inspiring careers. Polymode, the designers of this very book, are an American bicoastal, minority-owned design studio led by one African American man and another of Native American ancestry. On top of the fact that I've found their design work and knowledge to be impeccable, they also educate with their BIPOC design history classes. In the UK there is SMB Studios, founded by graphic designer Samuel Mensah whose typeface, Echelon, made it on to the Nike's athletic kit for Kevin Durant. And there is the incredibly well-edited, informative, and inspirational book *The Black Experience in Design: Identity, Expression & Reflection* that includes the work of six editors and over seventy designers, artists, curators, educators, students, and researchers, all with perspectives and design philosophies worthy of the immersion the book creates.

As it was then and as it is now, the response from the Black community has been to organize and unite. Black designers in Wacasey's time set up GAP (Group for Advertising Progress). One of GAP's aims was to pull together a database of contacts in the advertising field. It also placed people in roles (without acting as a formal recruiter). Now, Where are All the Black Designers? has taken up the mantle, with a job board on the site and callouts on Instagram. A weekend event by the platform in New York brought together the community and a virtual showcase exhibited the work of over 300 designers in an exhibition celebrating the "breadth and resilient nature in the Black creative experience."[221] Founded by David Rice, The Organization of Black Designers was established in 1990 with a focus on interior, fashion, and architecture, as well as graphic design. And in the UK we have Design Can, which combines campaigns, a platform of useful resources, monthly talks, workshops, and events to follow a manifesto ripe with the belief that change is afoot: "*Design Can* be more representative of the world it serves. *Design Can* be an industry for people of all backgrounds, abilities, ages and identities. *Design Can* be stronger with the talent that has been ignored for too long. *Design Can* disrupt the status quo, celebrate new voices, and tell untold stories. *Design Can* represent us all."[222] I join them in their buoyant assurances—*Design Can* do all the things they ask of it. History suggests that there is a river between can and will. I don't want someone in fifty years completing the exercise that I just did and signing off with the same breathy sigh: "Same, Same."

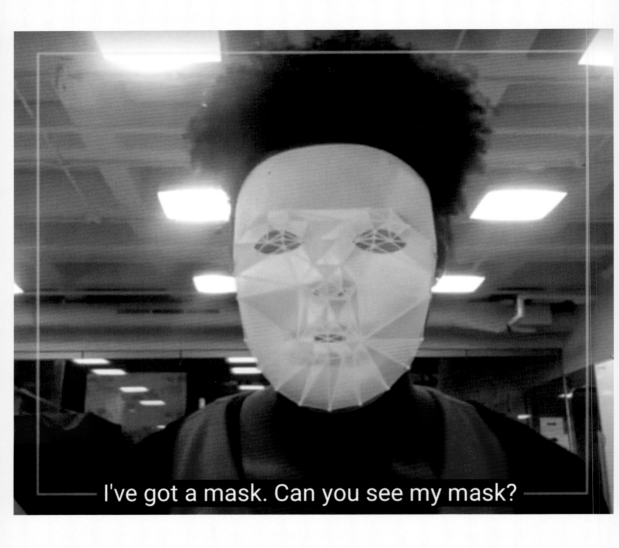

THE NEW FRONTIER
OF DE/IGN

So far, we have spoken at length about the positive impact of design. What is especially important is the hand Black designers have had in building a more equitable society through various routes such as visibility, creating spaces for Black people to live in, the establishment of organizations that support Black careers in design, and reframing the narrative around Black culture. As new technologies encroach on design spaces, fresh questions arise as to how design can operate in the domain of technology in a way that doesn't just minimize harm to Black people but allows the community of Black designers to flourish. In theory, as these technologies roll out at lightning speed in a time where no one can claim to be ignorant of racial bias (accepting or supportive, yes, but not ignorant), there should be checks and balances to ensure that there's a positive impact. Unfortunately, Zuckerberg's now famous motto, "Move fast and break things,"[223] doesn't seem to distinguish between people and software when employed by the tech world.

The "Tech" in A Vibe Called Tech provides a clue that the agency was initially born with technology in mind. I'd been on one of those long beach walks with my husband, James, where conversation takes strange roads, and we had gone into a fantasy land where we were pitching each other film scripts. One story was that killer robots would fulfill everyone's worst nightmares and come to murder us all, but the twist was that Black people would survive because killer robots wouldn't recognize us as human. There has been much pillow talk about who

OPPOSITE: Dr. Joy Buolamwini testing the 'Aspire Mirror' which only recognized her face when she wore a white mask.

owns this film idea, but I will concede that James was the first of the two of us to read somewhere that there was an issue with AI interpreting Black features. I assumed that he was a bit confused until doing a short Google search and discovering that this was in fact a very true, very real, non-fantasy film problem. Though now evolved into a full-service creative agency, A Vibe Called Tech began by raising awareness around the implications of technology for the Black community, and one of its first projects was a public engagement initiative highlighting issues of AI in the Black space through the lens of artists, designers, and photographers at the Tate Modern in London.

Since starting the work, I have been quoted in a *Dezeen* article saying that "technology's been coming for Black people since the beginning,"[224] and though I could have tempered the soundbite, the drama was justified given the circumstances—the evidence on this issue is fairly shocking. Let us begin with the facial recognition controversy that drew me into the space in the first place.

Joy Buolamwini, who describes herself as "a poet of code on a mission to show compassion through computation,"[225] now leads the Algorithmic Justice League (AJL), an organization using art and research to highlight the social implications of artificial intelligence. In 2015 Buolamwini conducted an experiment at the MIT Media Lab using facial recognition software to create an Aspire Mirror where individuals could look into a technological mirror and shape-shift into an animal, quotes, or symbols with the idea being that this would engender empathy by seeing ourselves as another. What actually happened is that the software—AI-enabled facial analysis technology—found it difficult to track Buolamwini's face. Buolamwini is a dark-skinned Black woman. One day, she put on a white mask and it tracked her face fine. When lighter-skinned colleagues tried out the mirror, also fine. I found this story on a TED Talk along with other stories of Google recognition software identifying Black people as gorillas,[226] as well as promises from the likes of IBM and Microsoft[227] to tackle the problem by improving data collection. Buolamwini has emphasised that the implications of this are hugely damaging: facial recognition is used to detect criminals; self-driving cars employ the technology to make sure that they don't run people over, and firms apply the software to help with hiring decisions. So, if Black faces aren't recognized at all or are misinterpreted in any way, with the previous scenarios as examples, we are at risk of, respectively, being falsely imprisoned, physically hurt, or unemployable. This discovery led to the birth of AJL and gives Buolamwini a platform to discuss the impact of facial recognition on civil rights and liberties with the US House Committee on Oversight and Government Reform. There's also a film to watch when you want to Netflix without the chill called *Code Bias*, where the whole story of facial bias is told and the threats it poses held up for scrutiny.

Since Buolamwini's TED Talk in 2017,[228] I've become aware of a number of activists and organizations who are deeply concerned about the capacity of technology design to act as yet another tool to undermine the Black community. One of those people is Charlton McIlwain, a professor of media, culture, and communication at New York University and author of *Black Software: The Internet & Racial Justice, from the AfroNet to Black Lives Matter*. In an article for *MIT Technology Review*, he looks at the history of technology in perpetuating the idea of people of color as problematic and asks whether we will "continue to design and deploy tools that serve the interests of racism and white supremacy,"[229] pointing to, among other things, credit scoring systems that disproportionately identify Black people as risky credit, stopping them from getting loans or buying homes. Data for Black Lives is another organization doing the work. Framed as "a movement of activists, organizers, and scientists committed to the mission of using data to create concrete and measurable change in the lives of Black people"[230] and founded by Yeshimabeit Milner, AI is a thread that they interrogate for racism with one article titled, "Data Capitalism and Algorithmic Racism"[231] that has become a microsite[232] where people can learn about the subject. Their concerns mirror that of Buolamwini and McIlwain, with nods to the gig economy where changes in algorithms can result in reduced pay for gig workers (who are disproportionately Black) and advertising systems that exclude Black users from seeing particular ads, or the proliferation of misinformation and racist content that spreads unhampered and bleeds into the real world.

As voices calling for change in technology design have become far reaching and more demanding, the tone of manifestos has been equally strident. One that I particularly enjoyed was presented by technology studio projects by IF Design, who I consulted with for a short time. There were ten principles in total ranging from Put Care First, where tech designers move away from delivering for individual or commercial interests, to Empowering Collective Agency, with the "radical inclusion of the most vulnerable."[233] But the one that stuck with me was the direction to Create Compassion at Scale. It states that "We have an opportunity to reshape AI and automation so they create *equity* and reinforce *civic commons*. People must be in control, always."[234]

The manifesto is not for Black people specifically but it embodies an approach to design in technology that addresses many Black issues around inclusion and equity. In some ways, new technologies such as AI, augmented reality, or even cyber security are very similar to the other forms of design that we've unpacked: Black people are in the minority and often go unconsidered. There are also a limited number of recognized and prominent Black technology designers. But the ways in which it differs from graphic design, fashion, and architecture is not only in the scale and speed of harm the technologies can cause but in the fact that they are in their relative infancy.

And it's in this tiny cove that I find hope. As we've trailed through the early twentieth century and the wrangling of designers to be seen and appreciated, the struggles of African architects to weave local culture into their buildings, or the confidence with which more recent designers have platformed and exposed the subtleties of Blackness, I see the reverberations of this work in how the potential damage of new technologies is being approached. There is a ferocity and enthusiasm with which we're teaching young Black children to code through initiatives like Black Boys Code and All Star Code. The push back on technology that is damaging Black communities is organized and continues to charge forward with intent as new technologies appear or circumstances exacerbate existing tools. The sense is that we are trying to get ahead of the damage before being enveloped by it.

There's a running joke (or mantra, depending on the gravity of the circumstances) shared between me and Lewis Gilbert, creative director of A Vibe Called Tech. We were in LA for work and decided to have brunch before visiting (the now sadly closed) The Underground Museum. It was one of those spots where people queue for too long and are too pleased with themselves for being there in the first place, and as we sat and ate our very special eggs, an old Black man stood outside the restaurant and started singing the line "When will we learn?" on repeat in a deep baritone. At first it was a bit surprising. The surprise soon turned into mild annoyance at the disruption to our life changing conversation but thirty minutes in, once it became clear that this man with gloriously clear skin and a curiously assured voice was not going to stop singing this line again and again, it became oddly emotional; if you listened carefully, you could hear heartbreak in his voice. "When will we learn?"—or more accurately, "When will *they* learn?—is what I ask now when I still see the legacy of racism in design, but my overwhelming feeling is that we, they, all of us are learning that our future cannot mirror the tawdry experiences of the past. I want to go back and tell the old man that we are learning. We are learning now.

Serwah Attafuah, *Into the Unknown*, 2023.
Digital 3D render.

ENDNOTES

149 David Rice quoted in, "The Black Experience in Design *is* Past, Present, *and* Future," https://blackexperienceindesign.com.

150 Simpson, E.S.C., & J.A. Weiner, *The Oxford Encyclopaedic English Dictionary* (Clarendon Press, 1989).

151 "We take a look at the etymology behind the word 'genius,'" *Colins Language Lovers Blog*, https://blog.collinsdictionary.com/language-lovers/we-take-a-look-at-the-etymology-behind-the-word-genius/.

152 Linda Nochlin, "Why have there been no great women artists?", *ARTnews*, May 30, 2015.

153 Cody Delistraty, "The Myth of the Artistic Genius," *The Paris Review*, January 8, 2020, https://www.theparisreview.org/blog/2020/01/08/the-myth-of-the-artistic-genius/.

154 Ibid.

155 Ibid.

156 John Stuart Mill, *Nature, The Utility of Religion, and Theism* (Longmans, 1923).

157 Linda Nochlin, "Why have there been no great women artists?", *ARTnews*.

158 Ibid.

159 Ibid.

160 Ibid.

161 Nancy Goldstein, *Jackie Ormes: The First African American Woman Cartoonist* (University of Michigan Press, 2008), pp. vii and 5.

162 "Meet Jackie Ormes and Torchy Brown," *New York Amsterdam News*, August 1, 2012, https://amsterdamnews.com/news/2012/08/01/meet-jackie-ormes-and-torchy-brown.

163 "BAME Young People at Greater Risk of Being in Unstable Employment," Next Steps, September 28, 2020, https://nextstepsstudy.org.uk/bame-young-people-at-greater-risk-of-being-in-unstable-employment.

164 "Roosevelt Opens Negro World Fair," *The New York Times*, July 5, 1940, https://timesmachine.nytimes.com/timesmachine/1940/07/05/112746030.html?pageNumber=15.

165 "The History of the Art Students League of New York," The Art Students League of New York, https://theartstudentsleague.org/history-art-students-league-new-york.

166 *American Negro Exposition, 1863–1940*, p. 1, https://libsysdigi.library.illinois.edu/OCA/Books2012-02/americannegroexp00amer/americannegroexp00amer.pdf.

167 Ibid, p. 9.

168 Daniel Schulman, "Design Journeys: Charles Dawson," AIGA, 2008, https://web.archive.org/web/20180924014255mp_/https://www.aiga.org/design-journeys-charles-dawson.

169 Chris Dingwall, "Race and Design of American Life: African Americans in Twentieth-Century Commercial Art," https://www.lib.uchicago.edu/media/documents/exrad-text.pdf.

170 Jontyle Theresa Robinson and Charles Austin Page, Jr., "Mending socks and tales of Africa," *The Christian Science Monitor*, October 15, 1987, https://www.csmonitor.com/1987/1015/umot.html.

171 "About Us," John Guggenheim Memorial Foundation, https://www.gf.org/about-us.

172 Pichaya Sudbanthad, "Emory Douglas: Biography," *AIGA Journal*, September 1, 2008, https://web.archive.org/web/20180707010716mp_/https://www.aiga.org/design-journeys-emory-douglas.

173 "Emory Douglas: The Art of the Black Panthers," Dress Code NY, https://vimeo.com/channels/staffpicks/128523144.

174 Addison Gayle, Jr., *The Black Aesthetic*, (Doubleday, 1971), p. xxiii.

175 Henry Louis Gates, Jr., "Black Creativity: On the Cutting Edge," *Time*, 1994, https://content.time.com/time/subscriber/article/0,33009,981564,00.html.

176 Addison Gayle, Jr., *The Black Aesthetic*, (Doubleday, 1971), pp. xxiii and xxiv.

177 Fine Acts, "12 Black Artists / 24 Protest Posters," https://fineacts.co/blm.

178 Jessica Werner Zack, "The Black Panthers advocated armed struggle. Emory Douglas' weapon of choice? The pen," *San Francisco Chronicle*, March 28, 2007, https://www.sfgate.com/entertainment/article/The-Black-Panthers-advocated-armed-struggle-2568057.php.

179 Jessie Garretson, "50 Movie Posters that Changed Entertainment Marketing," *Muse by Clio*, May 11, 2021, https://musebycl.io/film-tv/50-movie-posters-changed-entertainment-marketing.

180 Ibid.

181 Holly Willis, "Art Sims: Biography," AIGA Design Journeys, September 1, 2008, https://web.archive.org/web/20171024095727/http://www.aiga.org/design-journeys-art-sims.

182 Art Sims, "Black Movie Poster," The Tavis Smiley Show, NPR, August 19, 2003.

183 Art Sims in an email to author, August 23, 2022.

184 "Spike Lee's Do the Right Thing: Designer Art Sims and 11:24 Design," *StereoTyped*, November 1, 2009, http://thestereotypedblog.blogspot.com/2009/10/spike-lees-do-the-right-thing-designer-art.html.

185 "Are movie posters artwork? With Art Sims" (event description), St Bride Foundation, 2021, https://sbf.org.uk/whats-on/view/are-movie-posters-artwork/.

186 Burrell McBain Inc., *What Color is Black?*, advertisment, 1971. Collection of Emmett McBain Design Papers, The University of Illinois at Chicago, Richard J. Daley Library, Special Collections.

187 Tom Burrell in "DuSable to Obama: Chicago Black Metropolis | Achieving the dream: Advertising Black Pride," WTTW, https://interactive.wttw.com/dusable-to-obama/advertising-black-pride.

188 M. Chui, B. Gregg, S. Kohli, and S. Stuart III, "A $300 billion opportunity: Serving the emerging Black American Consumer," *McKinsey Quarterly*, August 6, 2021, https://www.mckinsey.com/featured-insights/diversity-and-inclusion/a-300-billion-dollar-opportunity-serving-the-emerging-black-american-consumer/.

189 Lydia Amoah, "The Black Pound Report," Backlight, 2022, https://www.backlight.uk/black-pound-report.

190 Graham Rapier, "Nike slides after trapping Colin Kaepernic as the new face of its 'Just Do It' ads," *Insider*, September 4, 2018, https://www.insider.com/nike-stock-price-colin-kaepernick-just-do-it-ads-2018-9.

191 Laura Snapes, "Puma 'glamorising drug dealing' with event featuring fake crack house," *The Guardian*, April 12, 2018, https://www.theguardian.com/music/2018/apr/12/puma-event-london-fake-crack-house-capital-crime.

192 Ibid.

193 Ibid.

194 "My Black Is Beautiful: The Women Behind the Movement," P&G Good Everyday, https://www.pggoodeveryday.com/good-news/black-is-beautiful-movement/.

195 Procter & Gamble: The Talk, July 25, 2017, https://youtube.com/watch?v=ovY6yjTe1LE.

196 Gabriel Arana, "Decades of Failure," *Columbia Journalism Review*, 2018, https://www.cjr.org/special_report/race-ethnicity-newsrooms-data.php/.

197 Ibid.

198 Emma Allen, "So, You Want to Be a New Yorker Cartoonist?", *The New Yorker*, June 6, 2021, https://www.newyorker.com/humor/daily-shouts/so-you-want-to-be-a-new-yorker-cartoonist.

199 Emily Flake, "We might not have any worshippers, but we're still a viable intellectual property.", *The New Yorker*, October 24, 2022.

200 Teresa Burns Parkhurst, "I know they should be invited to our house next, but can't we just give them cash and call it a day?", *The New Yorker*, October 24, 2022.

201 Nancy Goldstein, *Jackie Ormes: The First African American Woman Cartoonist* (University of Michigan Press, 2008), pp. vii and 5.

202 Liz Montague, "We've done all we can. It's out of our hands now.", *The New Yorker*, March 4, 2019.

203 Theresa Vargas, "A black female cartoonist brings her 'unique' take to the New Yorker," *The Washington Post*, February 1, 2020, https://www.washingtonpost.com/local/she-is-a-black-female-cartoonist-and-brings-a-unique-perspective-to-the-new-yorker/2020/02/01/c15b2f40-44a7-11ea-aa6a-083d01b3ed18_story.html.

204 Ibid.

205 Kayla Randall, "How Local Cartoonist Elizabeth Montague Creates Accessible, Reflective Art," *Washington City Paper*, September 19, 2019, https://washingtoncitypaper.com/article/178410/cartoonist-elizabeth-montague-makes-accessible-art.

206 Jacqueline Yoo, "Young, black, female Washington cartoonist speaks about diversity through her art", ABC News, February 14, 2020, https://abcnews.go.com/Politics/young-black-female-washington-cartoonist-speaks-diversity-art/story?id=68941786.

207 Ibid.

208 Theresa Vargas, "A black female cartoonist brings her 'unique' take to the New Yorker," *The Washington Post*, February 1, 2020, https://www.washingtonpost.com/local/she-is-a-black-female-cartoonist-and-brings-a-unique-perspective-to-the-new-yorker/2020/02/01/c15b2f40-44a7-11ea-aa6a-083d01b3ed18_story.html.

209 "About Us," Where are the Black Designers?, https://www.watbd.org/about-us.

210 *Design Census 2019: Understanding the state of design and the people who make it* (AIGA and Google, 2019), p. 14. https://web.archive.org/web/20201219115115/https://designcensus.org/data/2019DesignCensus.pdf

211 Natashah Hitti, "Design Can aims to disrupt UK's 'privileged' design industry," *Dezeen*, August 13, 2019 https://www.dezeen.com/2019/08/13/design-can-design-industry-uk-online-.

212 "The Black Experience in Graphic Design: 1968 and 2020," Letterform Archive, July 8, 2020, https://letterformarchive.org/news/view/the-black-experience-in-graphic-design-1968-and-2020.

213 Instagram post, July 15, 2020 @edward_enninful, https://www.instagram.com/p/CCrAm5Jld8l/?igshid=NTc4MTIwNjQ2YQ==.

214 "The Black Experience in Graphic Design: 1968 and 2020," Letterform Archive.

215 Ibid.

216 Ibid.

217 B. Hancock, J. Manyika, M. Williams, L. Yee, "The Black experience at work in charts," *McKinsey Quarterly*, April 15, 2021, https://www.mckinsey.com/featured-insights/diversity-and-inclusion/the-black-experience-at-work-in-charts.

218 "The Black Experience in Graphic Design: 1968 and 2020," Letterform Archive.

219 Eric Goldschein, "Racial Funding Gap Shows Black Business Owners Are Shut Out From Accessing Capital," *Nerdwaller*, January 8, 2021, https://www.nerdwallet.com/article/small-business/racial-funding-gap.

220 Gené Teare, "VC Funding to Black-Founded Startups Slows Dramatically as Venture Investors Pull Back," Crunchbase News, June 17, 2022, https://news.crunchbase.com/diversity/vc-funding-black-founded-startups/.

221 "About the Exhibition," Where are the Black Designers?, https://wherearetheblackdesigners.workingnotworking.com/about.

222 Design Can manifesto, https://www.design-can.com.

223 *Wired* Staff, "Mark Zuckerberg's Letter to Investors: 'The Hacker Way,'" *Wired*, February 1, 2012, https://www.wired.com/2012/02/zuck-letter/.

224 Natashah Hitti, "Technology's been coming for black people since the beginning' says Charlene Prempeh," *Dezeen*, October 28, 2020, https://www.dezeen.com/2020/10/28/a-vibe-called-tech-charlene-prempeh-interview/.

225 Barbican Centre, London, "Joy Buolamwini: examining racial and gender bias in facial analysis software," Google Arts & Culture, 2019, https://artsandculture.google.com/story/joy-buolamwini-examining-racial-and-gender-bias-in-facial-analysis-software-barbican-centre/BQWBaNKAVWQPJg?hl=en.

226 "Google apologises for Photo app's racist blunder," BBC News, July 1 2015, https://www.bbc.com/news/technology-33347866.

227 Alex Naibi, "Racial Discrimination in Face Recognition in Technology," Science in the News, October 24, 2020, https://sitn.hms.harvard.edu/flash/2020/racial-discrimination-in-face-recognition-technology/.

228 Joy Buolamwini, "How I'm fighting bias in algorithms," March 2017, https://www.ted.com/talks/joy_buolamwini_how_i_m_fighting_bias_in_algorithms.

229 Charlton McIlwain, "Of course technology perpetuates racism. It was designed that way," *MIT Technology Review*, June 3, 2020, https://www.technologyreview.com/2020/06/03/1002589/technology-perpetuates-racism-by-design-simulmatics-charlton-mcilwain/.

230 "About," Data for Black Lives, https://d4bl.org/about.html.

231 Data for Black Lives, "Data Capitalism and Algorithmic Racism," https://d4bl.org/reports/7-data-capitalism-and-algorithmic-racism.

232 Data for Black Lives, "Data Capitalism," https://datacapitalism.d4bl.org.

233 Society Centred Design, 2020, https://societycentered.design.

234 Ibid.

CREDITS

COLOPHON

Acknowledgements

Thank you to Courtney Mitchell for the many hours spent researching the designers and stories showcased here.

To Anna Godfrey who originally commissioned this book and Rochelle Roberts who picked up the baton and has been a wonderfully supportive and patient editor.

For reading and guiding, thank you, Sophie Lambert and the team at Curtis Brown.

To the team at Polymode for bringing the design of this book to life with unbridled enthusiasm and glorious talent.

Thank you, Laura Blakeman for championing the book and helping to take it out into the world.

Thank you to Chrystal Genesis for sparking the idea.

Thank you, Lewis Gilbert, for a trillion things but also for always picking up the phone.

Thank you, Chris Rokos, for providing space for me to write and for continually encouraging me to do so.

To James, for dealing with the early mornings, weekends, travel, late nights and for taking great care of me always.

Thank you to my Tiny Kings, Lucky and Story: I will always try my best.

© 2023 Prestel Verlag,
Munich · London · New York
A member of Penguin Random House
Verlagsgruppe GmbH
Neumarkter Strasse 28 · 81673 Munich

© for the text by Charlene Prempeh, 2023

A CIP catalogue record for this book is available from the British Library.

In respect to links in the book, the Publisher expressly notes that no illegal content was discernible on the linked sites at the time the links were created. The Publisher has no influence at all over the current and future design, content or authorship of the linked sites. For this reason the Publisher expressly disassociates itself from all content on linked sites that has been altered since the link was created and assumes no liability for such content.

Editorial direction: Rochelle Roberts

Copyediting: John Son

Design and typesetting: Polymode®, Randa Hadi, Brian Johnson, and Silas Munro, Los Angeles/Raleigh

Production: Corinna Pickart

Separations: Schnieber Graphik

Printing and binding: Alföldi Nyomda Zrt., Debrecen

Paper: Magno matt

Printed in Hungary

ISBN 978-3-7913-8847-2

www.prestel.com